Cotswolds
MountainBiking
20 Classic Rides

VERTEBRATE PUBLISHING

Design and production by Vertebrate Publishing, Sheffield
www.v-publishing.co.uk

Cotswolds
MountainBiking
20 Classic Rides

Written by
Tom Fenton

Cotswolds
MountainBiking
20 Classic Rides

VG Copyright © 2010 **Vertebrate Graphics Ltd and Tom Fenton**

VP Published by **Vertebrate Publishing**

ISBN 978-1-906148-14-0

Front cover photo: Tom Fenton descending from Bury Ramparts on Route 17.
Back cover photo: Stinchcombe Hill singletrack near Dursley.

Photography by **John Coefield**.

All maps reproduced by permission of Ordnance Survey on behalf of The Controller of Her Majesty's Stationery Office.
© Crown Copyright. 100025218

Design and production by Nathan Ryder.
www.**v-graphics**.co.uk

Mixed Sources
Product group from well-managed forests and other controlled sources
www.fsc.org   Cert no. DNV-COC-000087
© 1996 Forest Stewardship Council

Contents

ROUTE GRADES
▲ = MEDIUM ▲ = HARD ▲ = EXTREME (see page viii)

THE AUTHOR AND HAZEL WOODLAND TAKE A BREAK ABOVE ULEY

Introduction

Ask any mountain biker about the Cotswolds and they'll tell you about mud. I'm going to do the same.

My first Cotswolds ride was in the gloopy depths of winter. The ground was covered in a glue-like mire which stuck to everything. My bike doubled in weight. My wheels jammed. I slipped over, threw the bike into a ditch and sulked.

The following descent saved the day. I slid sideways between trees, slithered around corners and, when the inevitable finally happened, landed in the now welcome thick and soft mud.

Thanks to that descent, I ignored the mud and carried on riding in the Cotswolds. I've been out in proper 'winter wonderlands' when thick, clean snow has blurred the lines between bridleways, fields and lanes. I've kicked up smoky clouds of dust as I sped along sun-baked trails and I've ambled easily through summer evenings. I've hit the root-infested downhill runs at Leckhampton Hill as hard as I can and have definitely enjoyed a post-ride beer or two in village pub beer gardens.

I've had a lot of fun.

Do the same. Ignore the mud or pick a dry day and you'll find some great trails. There's riding in the Cotswolds for everybody. In the east, the rolling farmland, beautiful scenery and miles of easy tracks are unbeatable for a relaxed day out. Over to the west, the steep-sided hills and thick woodland create enough technical descents and tricky climbs to satisfy the most demanding rider. And if they don't, the tight corners, slick roots and big jumps on the downhill runs at Leckhampton Hill definitely will do.

Tom Fenton

Acknowledgements

Thanks to: Hazel Woodland for slogging through the mud with me; Karen Meacher for putting up with a kitchen full of muddy bikes; Matt Stott for correcting my pronunciation of Bibury; Jon at Zero G in Bristol for showing me around Lansdown and Neal Mundy and Pete Dodd for their Cotswold pub knowledge. This guide would have been much harder to write without your help!

Vertebrate would also like to thank Tom Fenton, Hazel Woodland and Jon Barton for being willing models for the photographs, particularly when asked by John to ride that last bit "just one more time...".

How to Use This Book

The Routes

Classics are fairly short (but not necessarily easy), **Epics** are a little longer and require a little more effort. **Enduros** step things up again and **Killers** are pretty self-explanatory.

The Cotswold Hills cover a massive area of land. Broadly speaking, the riding in the western side of the region is hillier, steeper and more technical, while the flatter eastern half features rolling hills and easier tracks. With the highest point in the Cotswolds soaring to a mighty 330m, you won't find huge descents and climbs here. What you will discover are short, steep ups and downs and riding ranging from easy farm tracks to field-edge bridleways and woodland singletrack, interspersed with sections of country lane.

Cotswolds Mud

Obviously, there's mud all over the world, but Cotswolds mud is special. It's thick, it's sticky and it turns fast, hard-packed trails into quagmires. Your favourite summer trail may be impassable in January, and vice versa. If you enjoy the esoteric challenge and charms of winter riding, head out anyway. If not, wait for the sun and the fast, dry trails – they more than make up for the muddy winters.

Grades

Routes, climbs and descents are graded blue, red and black, in a similar system to that used at several of the trail centres around the UK.

▲ = Easy ▲ = Moderate ▲ = Hard

Blue graded routes are generally shorter routes and are within reach of most MTBers, even newcomers, as well as the kind of thing you could do in a short day or when the weather's really foul. **Reds** are the kind of rides that won't actually take a full day, but you'll probably not want to do anything else once you've ridden them. And **Blacks** are those big and memorable days out that will demand endurance and some technical ability in places. These are the kind of routes to work up to.

The grades are based on average conditions – good weather and not too wet and muddy. In a drought the routes will feel easier, in the depths of winter, harder. Grades consider technicality, length, climbs, navigation, and remoteness – so one 'black' route might be a short all-out technical test while another could be a big endurance challenge with tricky navigation. As ever, these grades are subjective. How you find a particular route, downhill or climb will be dictated by your own levels of fitness and skill.

Directions & Accuracy

While every effort has been made to ensure accuracy within the directions in this guide, things change and we are unable to guarantee that every detail will be correct. Please treat stated distances as guidelines. **Please exercise caution if a direction appears at odds with the route on the ground. A comparison between direction and map should see you on the right track.**

Rights of Way

Countryside access in the UK hasn't been particularly kind to cyclists, although things are improving. We have 'right of way' on bridleways (blue arrows on signs) and byways (red arrows). However, having 'right of way' doesn't actually mean having the right of way, just that we're allowed to ride there – so give way to walkers and horse riders. We're also allowed to ride on green lanes and some unclassified roads, although the only way to determine which are legal and which aren't is to check with the local countryside authority. Obviously, cycle routes are also in.

The very understanding Forestry Commission generally allows cyclists to use its land (again, you'll need to check with them first to be sure). You must, however, obey all signs, especially those warning of forestry operations – a fully loaded logging truck will do more than scuff your frame...

Everything else is out of bounds (unless, of course, the landowner says otherwise). Riding illegally can upset walkers (who have every right to enjoy their day) and is, in many cases, technically classed as trespass (meaning you could be prosecuted for any damage caused). Not all tracks are signed, so it's not always obvious whether that great-looking trail you want to follow is an illegal footpath or a legal bridleway. That's why it's a good idea to carry a map with you on every ride.

The Bike

Generally any half-decent mountain bike (try and avoid a '£99 Special') will be absolutely fine for riding in the Cotswolds. If you have a cyclo-cross bike sitting in the shed, try taking that – many of the easier routes in the Cotswolds are not technical and would make great CX rides. For the harder routes, a full-suspension bike could add comfort and control, whilst a lightweight race bike might make the hills easier.

We would suggest that you choose your tyres carefully. If you have them, mud tyres with an aggressive and well-spaced tread pattern will cut through the clag, grip well and shed dirt quickly, vastly improving a winter ride. Failing that, fit the narrowest tyres you have – they'll improve the clearance of your bike and give the sticky mud less to cling to, keeping your wheels turning for longer.

Check everything's working – especially for harder riding. You won't be going uphill fast if your gears seize but may be quicker than planned if your brakes don't work. Pump the tyres up, check that nothing's about to fall off or wear through and check that everything that should be tight is tight.

Essential Kit

Helmet

"The best helmet is the one that you're wearing". Make sure it fits, you're wearing it correctly and that it won't move in a crash.

Clothing

You need to get your clothing right if you want to stay comfortable on a bike, especially in bad weather. The easiest way to do this is to follow a layering system. Begin with clothing made from 'technical' synthetic or wool fabrics that will wick the sweat away from your body and then dry quickly, keeping you dry and warm. Stay away from cotton – it absorbs moisture and holds onto it. If it's chilly, an insulating layer will keep you warm, and a wind/waterproof layer on the outside protects from the elements. Layers can then be removed or added to suit the conditions. Padded shorts are more comfortable, but the amount of lycra on display is down to you. Baggy shorts, full length tights and trousers are all available to match the conditions. Set off a little on the cold side – you'll soon warm up. Don't leave the warm clothes behind though, as the weather can turn quickly.

Gloves
Gloves ward off blisters and numb hands and help keep your fingers warm. They also provide a surprising amount of protection when you come off.

Footwear
Flat pedals/clips-ins – it's your call. Make sure you can walk in the shoes and that they have sufficient tread for you to do so. Consider overshoes if it's chilly.

Other essentials
As mentioned, take any necessary spares, tools, tube and pump, spare clothes, first aid kit, food and water. Stop short of the kitchen sink, as you'll still want to be able to actually ride your bike.

You'll need something to carry this lot in. We'd suggest a hydration pack, as they allow you to drink on the move and keep excess weight off the bike.

General Safety
The ability to read a map, navigate in poor visibility and to understand weather warnings is essential. Don't head out in bad weather, unless you're confident and capable of doing so.

Some of the routes described point you at tough climbs and steep descents that can potentially be very dangerous. Too much exuberance on a steep descent in the middle of nowhere and you could be in more than a spot of bother, especially if you're alone. Consider your limitations and relative fragility.

Be self-sufficient. Carry food and water, spares, a tube and a pump. Consider a first-aid kit. Even if it's warm, the weather could turn, so take a wind/waterproof. Think about what could happen on an enforced stop. Pack lights if you could finish in the dark.

If you're riding solo, think about the seriousness of an accident – you might be without help for a very long time. Tell someone where you're going, when you'll be back and tell them once you are back. Take a mobile phone if you have one, but don't expect a signal. And **don't** call out the ambulance because you've grazed your knee.

Riding in a group is safer (ambitious overtaking manoeuvres excepted) and often more fun, but don't leave slower riders too far behind and give them a minute for a breather when they've caught up. Allow extra time for a group ride, as you'll inevitably stop and chat. You might need an extra top if you're standing around for a while. Ride within your ability, make sure you can slow down fast and give way to other users. Bells might be annoying, but they work. If you can't bring yourself to bolt one on, a polite 'excuse me' should be fine. **On hot, sunny days, slap on some Factor 30+ and** ALWAYS WEAR YOUR HELMET!

In the Event of an Accident

In the event of an accident requiring immediate assistance: Dial 999 and ask for POLICE or AMBULANCE. If you can supply the services with a grid reference of exactly where you are it should help to speed up their response time.

Rules of the (Off) Road

1. Always ride on legal trails.
2. Ride considerately – give way to horses and pedestrians.
3. Don't spook animals.
4. Ride in control – you don't know who's around the next corner.
5. Leave gates as you find them – if you're unsure, shut them.
6. Keep the noise down and don't swear loudly when you fall off in front of walkers.
7. Leave no trace – take home everything you took out.
8. Keep water sources clean – don't take toilet stops near streams.
9. Enjoy the countryside and respect its life and work.

Planning Your Ride

1. Consider the ability/experience of each rider in your group. Check the weather forecast. How much time do you have available? Now choose your route.
2. Study the route description before setting off, and cross-reference it with the relevant map.
3. Bear in mind everything we've suggested about safety, clothing, spares and food and drink.
4. Get out there and get dirty.

Maps & Symbols

Ordnance Survey maps are the most commonly used, are easy to read and many people are happy using them. If you're not familiar with OS maps and are unsure of what the symbols mean, you can download a free map legend from **www.v-outdoor.co.uk**

We've included details of the relevant OS map for each route. To find out more about OS maps or to order maps please visit **www.ordnancesurvey.co.uk**

Here's a guide to the symbols and abbreviations we use on the maps and in our directions:

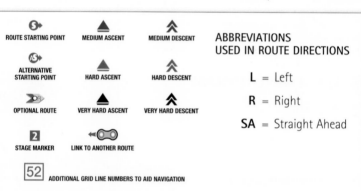

ROUTE STARTING POINT	**MEDIUM ASCENT**	**MEDIUM DESCENT**
ALTERNATIVE STARTING POINT	**HARD ASCENT**	**HARD DESCENT**
OPTIONAL ROUTE	**VERY HARD ASCENT**	**VERY HARD DESCENT**
STAGE MARKER	**LINK TO ANOTHER ROUTE**	
52 ADDITIONAL GRID LINE NUMBERS TO AID NAVIGATION		

ABBREVIATIONS USED IN ROUTE DIRECTIONS

L = Left

R = Right

SA = Straight Ahead

Cotswolds area map and **route finder**

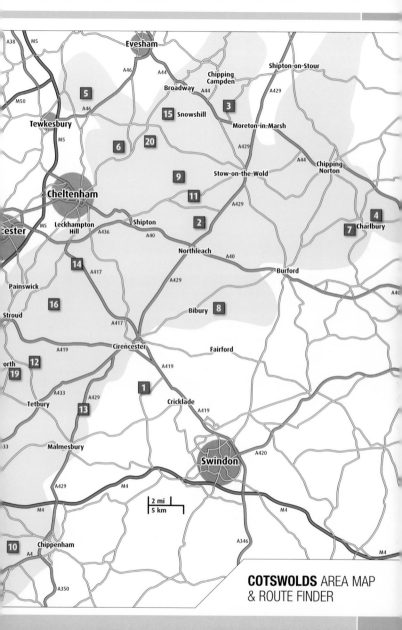

COTSWOLDS AREA MAP & ROUTE FINDER

SECTION 1

Classics

A quick blast after work, a night loop you can finish before your lights die, or a ride to squeeze in when time is short. That's a classic. They're not long, but that doesn't mean they're easy... Good, solid rides that all riders should enjoy.

Classics
sponsored by

www.sealskinz.com

LEAFY WOODLAND NEAR CLEVELEY (ROUTE 4)

WARNING

TREACHEROUS QUICKSAN

KEEP OUT

TAKE CARE AT THE COTSWOLD WATER PARK! (ROUTE 1)

Introduction

Almost entirely off-road and with virtually no climbing, this is a great easy route. Mixing wide trails with friendly singletrack, it manages to pull off the rare trick of being really good fun for less-experienced and faster riders alike. Weaving between lakes and running along old railway lines, the route is at its prettiest and most enjoyable in the summer, but copes well with Cotswold winters. Be aware that the Water Park is a popular spot and can get very busy on sunny summer weekends. It's easy to see why – this is the largest water park in the UK and has lots going on. The man-made lakes (formed through gravel extraction) offer a huge variety of activities, from sailing, canoeing and waterskiing to pony trekking, bird-watching and sun bathing on the beach!

The Ride

Leaving the car park, the route passes through fields on good tracks. It then nips across a quiet lane and begins to weave between lakes on seemingly endless stretches of wide singletrack. Watch out – *'Warning! Quicksand!'* signs border the trail (sadly, I've never spotted any hungry pits of bottomless sand). Safety is soon reached on the good, hard and dead-straight cycleway that runs up the east side of the Park. This ducks under railway arches as it runs northwards to the village of South Cerney. Stop for a pint or an ice lolly before heading out along more undemanding singletrack and a short section of road to return to the car park.

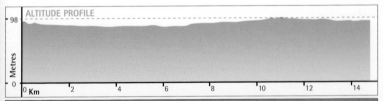

ALTITUDE PROFILE

COTSWOLD WATER PARK   **GRADE:** ▲

TOTAL DISTANCE: 15KM » **TOTAL ASCENT**: 30M » **TIME**: 1–2 HOURS » **START/FINISH**: CAR PARK OFF THE B4696
START GRID REF: SU 052952 » **SATNAV**: SOUTH CERNEY » **OS MAP**: LANDRANGER 163
PUB: ELIOTT ARMS, SOUTH CERNEY, TEL: 01285 860 215 » **CAFÉ**: USUALLY AN ICE CREAM VAN AROUND

Directions – Cotswold Water Park

❻ Bear **L** from the back of the car park. Follow bridleway signs across the field and through the narrow gap. Bear **R** across fields on obvious tracks. Follow the track as it turns and runs parallel to the road. Continue **SA** through the gap in the hedge as the track ends and follow bridleway signs **SA** through a second hedge onto a wide track beside a lake. Cross the road, don't sink in the quicksand, and follow the bridleway for 700m before turning **L** on to the Thames Path.

2 Meander between lakes on wide singletrack. Go through a gate and join a wider track, follow this to a larger gate and turn **R** to follow bridleway signs across a wooden bridge. At the T-junction, turn **R**.

3 At the second T-junction, turn **L**. Follow the wide track under railway bridges to the road. Go **SA** over the road and under the arches into the car park. Continue through this on the wide track to the left. At the road, keep **L**, off the road and on the cycleway. When this ends, cross the road onto a signed cycle path. Follow this through low arches and behind houses to the road.

4 Turn **L** into South Cerney. At the T-junction, turn **R** towards Ewan/Ashton Keynes. After 150m, turn **L** onto Ashton Lane. As the houses end, turn **R** onto a narrow bridleway. Follow this to the road and turn **L**.

5 At the crossroads with the B4696, turn **L**. Take care – this can be busy – and join the cycle path on the pavement after 100m. Follow this to the car park.

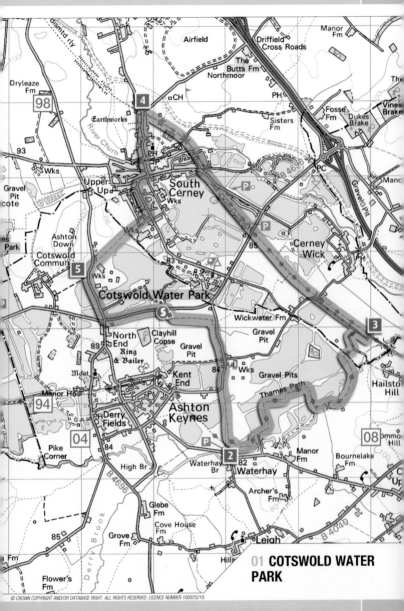

01 COTSWOLD WATER PARK

02 Cold Aston

13km

Introduction

Fields of sheep, pleasant countryside and easy–but–enjoyable riding. This is a winner if you're after a short/quick/easy (delete as appropriate) ride. Similar in distance to the Water Park route, this is a noticeably harder ride. While never difficult, there are loose tracks, rutted fields and a couple of steep sections to contend with – it's a proper bike ride! Despite crossing a couple of fields which can get a bit soggy in wet weather, the route does well in winter. Set right in the middle of the Cotswolds, the scenery is every bit as picturesque as you might expect and the villages along the way – Hazleton and Cold Aston – add a bit of rural charm, which is always nice.

The Ride

Leave Cold Aston on the road, spinning easily past farms and into the countryside. The tarmac surface soon begins to deteriorate, rapidly turning into a wide stone-based track. This runs all the way to Hazleton via a couple of fast descents and taxing climbs. It also passes through the outskirts of Turkdean – a village with roots tracing back to Roman times. Dropping away from Hazleton the return leg of the ride begins, rattling across farmland to Notgrove. From here, a particularly pleasing bridleway straight-lines its way up a narrow strip of woodland, dodging roots and ploughing through piles of leaves all the way back to Cold Aston.

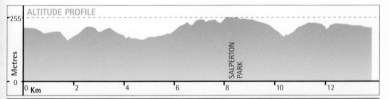

COLD ASTON — **GRADE:** ▲

TOTAL DISTANCE: 13KM » **TOTAL ASCENT**: 300M » **TIME**: 1–2 HOURS » **START/FINISH**: COLD ASTON VILLAGE CENTRE
START GRID REF: SP 129197 » **PARKING**: ON-STREET, COLD ASTON » **SATNAV**: GL54 3BN » **OS MAP**: LANDRANGER 163
PUB: THE PLOUGH, COLD ASTON, TEL: 01451 821 459 » **CAFÉ**: BRING SANDWICHES

02 COLD ASTON — GRADE ▲   9

Directions – Cold Aston

⊙➤ Head west out of Cold Aston towards Notgrove. Turn **L** as you leave the village and follow the lane through the farm onto a dirt track. Follow this, ignoring all turnings, to the road in Turkdean.

2 At the T-junction, turn **R** and then immediately **L**, passing through the farm and through a gate onto a wide track. Follow this track into and along the valley to two gates. Go through the left-hand gate and climb gradually to the village of Hazleton.

3 Once in Hazleton, turn **R** at the first road junction and go **SA** at the crossroads. Go **SA** over the house drive and follow grassy tracks along field edges. Drop through woods and keep **SA** up the obvious track. Go through the gate and turn **R** at the T-junction.

4 Follow the wide track past the houses and continue **SA** into fields. Drop **SA** to a gate and turn **R** beyond it, aiming for a lone tree. Go through next gate and turn **L** uphill, following grassy tracks and a tarmac lane to the road.

5 Turn **L** and then **R** to Notgrove. Continue **SA** at the road junction and follow the road to a sharp hairpin formed by a stone wall. Follow bridleway signs through a wide metal gate and drop across the field beyond before climbing to a second gate. Turn **R** and then **L** onto an obvious bridleway running through the narrow woods. At the road, turn **R** and ride back to Cold Aston.

02 COLD ASTON

03 Blockley & Broad Campden

21km

Introduction

Exploring the north-eastern corner of the Cotswolds, this route follows entertaining trails through pretty villages, showing off attractive views as it goes. A couple of good, contrasting descents (one fast and open, one narrower and slower) and two significant climbs complete the route. Tracing a circle around Blockley, it's not a technically difficult ride, but with fast descents, bumpy fields and aforementioned climbs, it's not one for complete beginners either. As you come to expect from the Cotswolds, the rolling farmland and picturesque villages (check out the thatched roofs in Broad Campden!) add significantly to the attraction of the route. Blockley itself is a former centre of silk production. With winding streets between yellow stone buildings and an ancient Norman church, it makes an attractive start and finish to the day.

The Ride

Winding along narrow streets of yellow-brick buildings, the roads through Blockley make a particularly charming start to the ride. The ride proper kicks in almost before leaving the houses, with a lengthy climb on easy tracks through Bourton Woods. This ends on a fast and busy road – so take care. Luckily, you're not on this for long, soon turning off to run along field-edge tracks and through woods to the top of the first significant descent of the route. Pause for a moment and admire the view out over Chipping Campden. The long, straight and open descent is predictably fast, running into the village of Broad Campden. A stretch along the road, more good-looking villages and a fair chunk of climbing lead to the route's finale – the descent off Cadley Hill. Dropping to Blockley, this is fast, muddy fun and offers an impressive view of the village below – if you remember to stop and look!

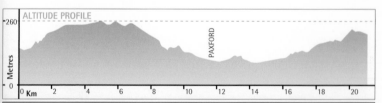

ALTITUDE PROFILE

260

Metres

0

| 0 Km | 2 | 4 | 6 | 8 | 10 | 12 | 14 | 16 | 18 | 20 |

PAXFORD

BLOCKLEY & BROAD CAMPDEN

GRADE: ▲

TOTAL DISTANCE: 21KM » **TOTAL ASCENT**: 400M » **TIME**: 2–4 HOURS » **START/FINISH**: BLOCKLEY VILLAGE SHOP
START GRID REF: SP 164348 » **SATNAV**: GL56 9BB » **PARKING**: ON-STREET IN BLOCKLEY » **OS MAP**: LANDRANGER 151
PUB: GREAT WESTERN ARMS, BLOCKLEY, TEL: 01386 700 362 » **CAFÉ**: BLOCKLEY VILLAGE SHOP AND CAFE

Directions – Blockley & Broad Campden

➎ With your back to the village shop, turn **L** and, ignoring turnings, wind along the High Street to a gate. Go **SA** onto a wide dirt track and, again ignoring turnings, climb to the road. **Take care** – this is a fast and busy road.

2 Turn **R** along the road. After 1km, turn **R** onto a tarmac lane signed as a bridleway. Go through the trees and, after a short distance, turn **L** to follow vague tracks along the field edge. Go **SA** over the lane and continue along more field edges.

3 Go **SA** over the road and ride into the woods. Ignoring turnings, climb steeply out up the track and out of the trees. As the track bends right, go **SA**, following bridleway signs onto field-edge tracks. In the trees, turn sharp **R** and, after 100m, sharp **L**. Go through the gate and follow more vague tracks **SA** across fields and between small trees to the road.

4 Turn **R**, then **R** again onto a wide dirt track. Keep **SA** through the gate as the track bends right and descend to Broad Campden. Turn **R**, then quickly turn **L** onto a road signed *Unsuitable for Vehicles*. At the T-junction, turn **L** and follow the road downhill out of the village.

5 After 1km, turn **L** onto a signed bridleway. Pass through fields and cross the railway. As you approach houses, turn **R** across a small bridge and follow grassy tracks to the road. Turn **L** and ride into Paxford, then take the first **R** and ride out of the village. Follow the road as it narrows between houses and shortly afterwards, turn **R** onto a wide track. Keep **R** at the farm, go under the railway and then keep **L** at the fork.

6 At the road, turn **L** and climb into Aston Magna. Once in the houses, take the second **R**, signed *Batsford* and continue climbing. Keep **SA** over the first crossroads and then turn **R** at the second.

7 As the climb eases and the road bends left, go **SA** through a gate onto a signed bridleway. Bear **L** across the field and follow field edges to gates. Still following bridleway signs, go through the right-hand gate and follow singletrack downhill. Pass to the **L** of the barn and drop into Blockley. At the T-junction, turn **R** and then take the second **L**. Turn **L** at the T-junction to return to the start of the ride.

03 BLOCKLEY & BROAD CAMPDEN

Introduction

A strangely satisfying ride. It's not technical and doesn't take long but the riding's good and enjoyable and runs through some lovely countryside. Almost an 'off-road road-ride' (with a few bits of singletrack thrown in...), this is one of those routes where you can get into a nice pedally rhythm, fill your bloodstream with endorphins and ride off into the sunset. With a pub at the halfway point, it's a worthwhile choice if you want a cruisy day out in the country, but would also be great for blasting around for a couple of hours at a gratifyingly fast pace.

The Ride

The ride moves off-road before even leaving town, following a good track out past the houses. Grassy trails and field edges climb gently up to the Wychwood Way, from where dirt tracks run north towards Chipping Norton. With no real gradients to speak of, you can get into a great rhythm as you speed along. The track soon narrows to wide singletrack with the odd root and low branch to dodge, before swinging right onto grassy tracks along the bottom of a golf course. More good tracks, bumpy fields and a short but fast and fun descent lead to Enstone and, if you want it, the Crown Inn. Singletrack, a brief section of road (alongside one of the most perfect examples of a meandering river you'll ever see) and a stretch along easy tracks lead back to the Wychwood Way and a fast run down to Charlbury.

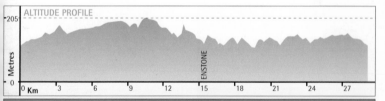

ALTITUDE PROFILE

Metres — 205, 0 — ENSTONE

Km: 0, 3, 6, 9, 12, 15, 18, 21, 24, 27

CHARLBURY CLASSIC   **GRADE:** ▲

TOTAL DISTANCE: 29KM » **TOTAL ASCENT**: 350M » **TIME**: 1.5-3 HOURS » **START/FINISH**: SPENDLOVE CENTRE CAR PARK, CHARLBURY » **START GRID REF**: SP 358196 » **SATNAV**: OX7 3PQ » **PARKING**: CAR PARKS IN CHARLBURY
OS MAP: LANDRANGER 164 & 163 » **PUB**: CROWN INN, CHURCH ENSTONE, TEL: 01608 677 262; THE ROSE AND CROWN, CHARLBURY, TEL: 01608 810 103; THE BULL INN, CHARLBURY, TEL: 01608 810 689 » **CAFÉ**: SHOPS IN CHARLBURY; CAFE IN NEWSAGENTS

04 **CHARLBURY CLASSIC**

Directions – Charlbury Classic

❺➤ From the Spendlove Centre car park, turn **L** onto Enstone Road. As you reach the outskirts of Charlbury, turn **R** onto Hundley Way. Keep **SA** as the lane becomes dirt. Climb field edges and turn **L** at the T-junction with a wide track. Keep **SA** upon joining tarmac and then branch **R** onto a marked byway as the road bends left.

2 Follow the obvious track, crossing two roads. At the third, bear **R** along the road. After 1.5km, turn **R** onto a signed bridleway.

3 Continue **SA**, ignoring all turnings, to the golf course. Turn **R** through a narrow gate at the bottom of the course and follow bridleway signs to the main road. Bearing slightly **L**, go **SA** over the road into Chalford Park Barns.

4 Go past the buildings, through a gate and keep **SA** along the obvious track. Following bridleway signs, turn **R** at the first T-junction and **L** at the second, heading towards a farm. Pass through the buildings and turn **L** at the T-junction. Almost immediately bear **R** through a narrow gate in the hedge signed *Bull in Field*. Turn **R** across the field to a second gate and go **SA** through this and into the woods.

5 Drop down the obvious track, cross the river and bear **R** (in effect **SA**) up the wide bridleway on the far side. Upon leaving the woods, bear **R** across open ground in front of the buildings and follow the field edge to a gate. Cross the river, climb a short rise and turn **L** to pass through another gate. Climb across the field and through the woods. Continue **SA** through the farm onto grass tracks. Cross fields, keep to the right-hand side of the wall as you reach the allotments and drop to the road junction. Turn **L**, off the main road, into Enstone.

6 Follow the road downhill and then up past the pub. Turn **R** just before the national speed limit signs onto a narrow lane marked as *Unsuitable for Heavy Goods Vehicles*. At the T-junction, go **SA** across the road onto a narrow bridleway. Follow this to the road. Keep **R** at the triangular road junction and take the next **L**. After 200m, turn **R** onto a signed bridleway by a telephone box. At the road, turn **L**.

7 Take the second lane on the **L**, signed *Radford*. Drop downhill, admire the meandering stream and then turn **R** onto a grassy bridleway just before the road crosses the river. Climb through the woods and keep **SA**, along field edges and then good tracks, to the road. Turn **L** and then take the second **R** towards Ditchley Park. Keep **R** at the first fork and **L** at the second. At the T-junction, turn **R**, and, after 400m, turn **R** again onto a wide track.

8 After 1km, turn **L**, passing in front of the house on good tracks. **Easy to miss**: Cross fields, follow the track to the left and then quickly turn **R** onto a signed bridleway. Keep **SA** at to the road and turn **R** at the T-junction. Turn **L** at the crossroads and retrace your steps to the car park.

05 Bredon Hill

Introduction

With two singletrack descents and a couple of big climbs, this is a great ride that should take about two hours to complete. Tracing a figure-of-eight over the top of Bredon Hill, you can add amazing views to the appeal of the route. Taken with a relaxed approach to the climbs and a little caution on the descents, this is a relatively easy ride. Carry a bit more speed downhill, work hard on the ups and suddenly things are a little more exciting! Bredon Hill itself is an interesting place. Besides the views and the riding, there's a herd of deer up there, an Iron Age fort and a tower whose stature boosts the height of the hill past the 1,000ft mark. You may also be fascinated to know that the Celtic 'Bre', the old English 'don' and the obvious 'hill' all mean the same thing...

The Ride

The ride begins with a short cruise along the main road through Kemerton. Make the most of it – by the time you leave the houses you'll be slogging away up a steep road climb. Tarmac soon gives way to dirt and grass, but the climb continues to the top of the hill. A brilliant high speed descent through the woods drops off the other side onto open ground. Technically easy, it's still great fun. A short road spin and an often-muddy track past a pig farm(!) lead into Ashton under Hill, from where a big climb on road, rock and grass takes you back up the hill with ever-improving views. Good trails lead over the flat summit onto wide swooping singletrack, before fast, open trails plummet towards Kemerton. A great little ride.

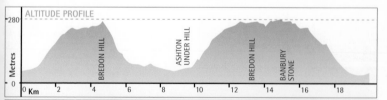

BREDON HILL **GRADE:** ▲

TOTAL DISTANCE: 20KM » **TOTAL ASCENT**: 550M » **TIME**: 2-3 HOURS » **START/FINISH**: THE CROWN, KEMERTON
START GRID REF: SO 945371 » **SATNAV**: GL20 7HP » **PARKING**: ON-STREET IN KEMERTON » **OS MAP**: LANDRANGER 150
PUB: THE CROWN, KEMERTON, TEL: 01386 725 293 » **CAFÉ**: NONE ON ROUTE

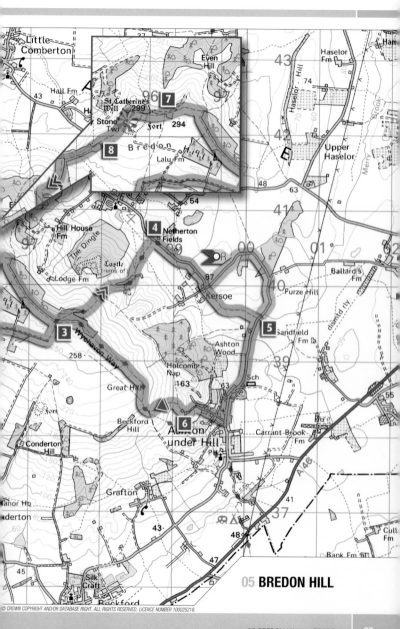

05 **BREDON HILL**

➊ With your back to The Crown in Kemerton, turn **R** and follow the main road out of the village. Immediately after the church, turn **L**. Ignoring all turnings, climb to a gate. Go through the gate and fork **R**, following a signed bridleway off the main track into the woods. Follow this through a gate and onto a grassy track.

2 Continue **SA** onto a wide dirt track and follow this uphill and around to the **R**. Go **SA** at the crossroads, and then continue **SA** onto dirt when the lane swings left. Follow this **SA** and then around to the **L**, climbing once more. Go **SA** through gates, over the track junction and into the woods.

3 Drop through the woods, going **SA** (slightly **L**) at the track junction. Following bridleway markers, continue into open ground and head **SA**, downhill. Reaching a couple of trees, bear **R** across a small, low, wooden bridge. Crest a small rise and turn **L** after a second bridge. Go through the gate and follow the right-hand edge of the field to the road.

4 Turn **R**. After 1km, turn **R** and then immediately **L** onto a bridleway*. Follow this, keeping close to the stream, to the road.

*Optional Route – Wet weather route
OR From **4**, stay on the main road and rejoin the route at **5**, riding into Ashton under Hill.

5 Turn **R** and ride into Ashton under Hill. Turn **R** up Cottons Lane. Ignoring turnings, climb until the road ends at stables. Bear **R** through a gate to the right and climb steeply. Keep **L** at the fork.

6 Climb up the field. As the gradient eases, move **L** onto a more obvious track and go through the gate. Shortly after this, bear **R** off the track following bridleway signs, and climb through another gate. Turn **R** and follow the edge of the field to the top of the hill. Keep **SA** alongside the woods, following the track along the edge of the trees and crossing your earlier route. Ignore turnings to the end of the woods and then go **SA** through the gate. Keep to the top of the field and follow the vague track around to the left.

7 Go through the gate onto open ground and, keeping close to the wall on your right, continue **SA** towards the tower. Go past the tower, through gates and into the woods.

8 Follow singletrack roughly **SA** through the woods (keep in the woods and on the singletrack) and then turn sharp **L** immediately beyond the trees. Ignoring turnings, descend over grass and then good tracks to the road. Follow the road to a T-junction and turn **L** to return to Kemerton.

SECTION

Epics

Getting longer, Epics require that bit more time and effort. The difficulty varies but all feature a mix of fast, technical and tough riding that covers some interesting ground and is not to be underestimated. Allow a few hours and enjoy some of the best riding the Cotswolds has to offer.

Epics
sponsored by

www.muc-off.com

CLIMBING UP TO THE GOLF COURSE NEAR NAUNTON (ROUTE 9)

NEAR SHORTHAMPTON (ROUTE 7)

Introduction

Starting from the bustling tourist hotspot of Winchcombe, the ride runs up Cleeve Hill, which, at a mighty 330m, is the highest point in the Cotswolds. Unfortunately, no bridleways run to the very top, so you'll have to settle for the views from slightly lower down. Don't worry – these stretch to Wales! The ride is more than just a pretty vista though, cramming a couple of cracking descents and some stiff climbs into its 20km length. It darts up and down the hill on trails that are very different in character. Ranging from the fast and loose to the stony-faced and wooden, they all offer fantastic riding. A couple do suffer badly in the winter, becoming much harder work, but pick your day carefully and fast trails and expansive views await!

The Ride

The spin past Sudeley Castle and up the valley beyond is a particularly civilised start to the day. Enjoy it, as the climb at the far end kicks you out of bed and sets your legs on fire. A brief stint on the road, an easy track and a grassy field lead to a wide-open descent off Cleeve Hill. You'll want to pause on the way down this, as the views are something else! Singletrack leads up onto Cleeve Common, from where a brilliant descent drops the entire height of the hill, bouncing over roots and weaving between trees. Sadly, this gets very muddy in the winter. There's a short cut highlighted, but I'd wait for dry weather myself. A big slog up the main road follows, but with a pub, more views and a good descent waiting, just get it on with it. After a quick skip across grassland, the reward is an ever-accelerating rocky blast back to Winchcombe.

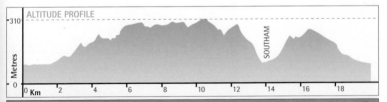

ALTITUDE PROFILE

Metres

310

0

0 Km   2   4   6   8   10   12   14   16   18

SOUTHAM

WINCHCOMBE & CLEEVE HILL   **GRADE:** ▲

TOTAL DISTANCE: 20KM » **TOTAL ASCENT:** 600M » **TIME:** 2-4 HOURS » **START/FINISH:** T-JUNCTION IN WINCHCOMBE CENTRE
START GRID REF: SP 025283 » **SATNAV:** WINCHCOMBE » **PARKING:** PAY AND DISPLAY IN WINCHCOMBE
OS MAP: LANDRANGER 163 » **PUB:** WHITE HART, WINCHCOMBE, TEL: 01242 602 359; ROYAL OAK, GRETTON, TEL: 01242 604 999;
LOTS MORE IN WINCHCOMBE » **CAFÉ:** JURI'S TEA ROOM, TEL: 01242 602 469; SEVERAL MORE IN WINCHCOMBE

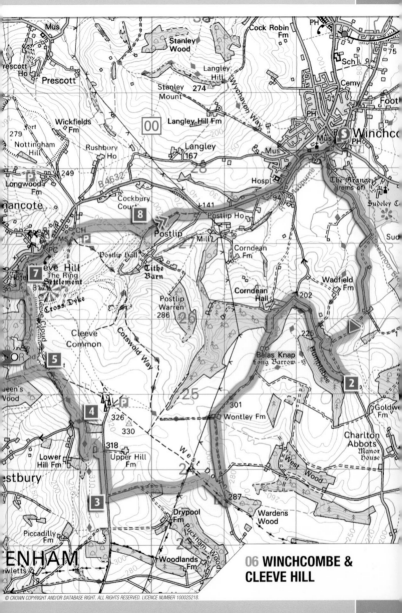

06 WINCHCOMBE & CLEEVE HILL

Directions – Winchcombe & Cleeve Hill

➊ From the main T-junction in Winchcombe formed by North Street and the High Street, turn **R** (if you're on North Street) and head towards Cheltenham. Take the second **L** onto Vineyard Street, following signs for *Sudeley Castle*. Keep **R** past the castle and follow the lane along the valley. At the end, turn **R** through a gate onto an obvious track. Climb steeply to the road.

2 Turn **R**, ride into the woods and turn **L**. Keep **L** at the fork and ride **SA** through the farm onto a rough track. Follow this to a small car park. Just before reaching it, turn **R** through a gate into a grassy field. After 400m, turn **L** through a second gate and ride along field edges (muddy in winter) to join a wide track. Ignoring turnings, follow this to the road.

3 Turn **R** and, after 500m, turn **L** through a gate onto a signed bridleway running into the nature reserve. Admire the view for a minute and then drop around the woods on obvious tracks. Swing to the **R** around a large switchback and go **SA** through the gate. At the T-junction, turn **L** and continue to descend.

4 (**Very easy to miss**) After about 75m, turn **R** onto singletrack. If you hit a technical, rocky section of track, you've missed the turning, so hang a U-turn and have a more careful look. Climb singletrack to a multi-track junction. Go **SA**, crossing the gully, and continue climbing, following bridleway signs, to a gate.

5 Go through the gate and keep **L**, hugging the fence. Bear **L** down the obvious rocky descent and trend **L** across the plateau*, following vague tracks to a gate leading into the woods. Fly or squelch – depending on the season – down an entertaining descent to the road.

*Optional Route – Wet weather route

OR Keep **R** across the plateau, crest a small rise and turn **R** onto the obvious track behind the houses. Follow this to a small car park by a cattle grid and rejoin the directions at **7**.

6 **Take care** – the road can be busy. Turn **R** and climb for 1km to the Rising Sun pub. Turn **R** immediately before this onto Rising Sun Lane and cross the cattle grid into a small car park. Turn **L**.

7 Follow good tracks across the grassy common. Keep **R** past the lone building up a short, steep rise and follow the obvious track past the golf course. Keep **SA** through the gate.

8 At a T-junction after a second gate turn **L**, pass through a third gate and rattle down to join the main road. Turn **R** to return to Winchcombe.

Introduction

Open countryside, good trails and pretty villages make up this easy-going exploration of the eastern Cotswolds. With no real hills to speak of, the climbs are gradual and the descents fast and uncomplicated. Rolling through open farmland, the views from the ride stretch out over the wide fields that create the surrounding countryside. Although the route remains relatively rideable in winter, warm, dry and lazy weather seems to fit it better. There are a couple of villages with pubs at the two-thirds/three-quarters point of the ride, although sadly, no cafes.

The Ride

The ride begins on the road, climbing gently from Charlbury to Spelsbury. A short but fun descent then drops briefly into woodland, before grassy trails climb to the village of Chadlington. Following a long, straight byway, the route heads north out of the village through fields. Pause to admire the steadily growing view behind you and then continue to the road. After a quick spin along quiet lanes, a wide bridleway drops gently alongside Sarsgrove Wood. This is one of those trails where pedalling is effortless and speed comes easily. The route then swings south, heading through open countryside to Shipton under Wychwood. From here, the return leg of the ride takes in some fast, field-edge descents and open trails as it carries you to the final sweeping descent towards Charlbury.

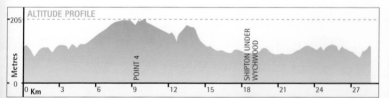

ALTITUDE PROFILE

205

Metres

POINT 4

SHIPTON UNDER WYCHWOOD

0 Km   3   6   9   12   15   18   21   24   27

CHARLBURY & SHIPTON   GRADE: ▲

TOTAL DISTANCE: 28KM » **TOTAL ASCENT**: 350M » **TIME**: 2–4 HOURS » **START/FINISH**: SPENDLOVE CENTRE CAR PARK, CHARLBURY » **START GRID REF**: SP 358196 » **SATNAV**: OX7 3PQ » **PARKING**: CAR PARKS IN CHARLBURY **OS MAP**: LANDRANGER 163 » **PUB**: CROWN INN, CHURCH ENSTONE, TEL: 01608 677 262; THE ROSE AND CROWN, CHARLBURY, TEL: 01608 810 103; THE BULL INN, CHARLBURY, TEL: 01608 810 689 » **CAFÉ**: SHOPS IN CHARLBURY; CAFE IN NEWSAGENTS

07 CHARLBURY & SHIPTON

Directions – Charlbury & Shipton

S Leave the car park and turn **L**. Turn **L** at the crossroads and then **R** at the T-junction. Follow the road into Spelsbury and fork **L** towards Chadlington.

2 After 350m, turn **R** onto a signed bridleway. Keep **L** as the track forks and then stay **L** across a small clearing to a gate. Go through this and climb through the field to the road. Go **SA** onto a small lane and, after 50m, turn **L** onto a bridleway.

3 At the road, turn **R** into Chadlington. Shortly after entering the village, turn **R** up Church Lane. Keep **SA** on to a wide track as the road bends to the left and ride away from the houses. At the road, turn **L**.

4 Turn **L** at the crossroads with the main road. Keep **R** at the fork and then turn **R** onto a signed bridleway leading into the woods. Keep **SA** onto the lane and go **SA** at the crossroads. After 300m, turn **L** through gates. Keep **SA** across the large courtyard on to the obvious track. Follow this, ignoring turnings, out across open ground. Keep going **SA**, passing through some huge ancient stone posts and across a good track. At the bridleway junction, just after a large hedge, turn **R** and speed downhill on grassy tracks. Turn **L** at the road and then take the next **R**.

5 Climb the lane for 1.4km, pass under the railway and turn **L** onto a grassy bridleway. Cross the field and turn **L** as you reach the far side. Go through the gate and turn **R** onto a wide track. Follow this into Shipton under Wychwood (pubs if you want them!). At the road, turn **L** and ride out of the village.

6 After about 1km, cross the railway and turn **R** onto a bridleway just after the national speed limit signs (it looks as if you are riding into the garden of Little Acorns). Cross the railway and follow singletrack to a small lane. Follow this to the main road and turn **L**. At the T-junction, turn **R** and then take the first **L**, signed *Village Shop*. As the road bends left, turn **R** through a gate onto a signed bridleway.

7 Go **SA** diagonally across the field. As you enter a second field, turn back **R** on yourself and ride around the sides of this field to the opposite corner. Then follow vague tracks and bridleway signs roughly **SA** to the road. Follow the lane to the main road, turn **L** and then quickly turn **R** onto another bridleway. Follow obvious tracks to the road and go **SA**. At the T-junction, go **SA** onto a signed bridleway. At the road, turn **L** and climb back to Charlbury. Turn **L** at the T-junction, take the next **R** and follow the road back to the start.

Introduction

It could be argued that a nineteenth century architect who dabbled in art, poetry and textile design would know beauty when he saw it. So, when the man in question, William Morris, described Bibury as the 'prettiest village in England', you can safely assume that the village will make a rather fine start to a ride. With roots stretching to back to Saxon times, Bibury has a trout farm, a Saxon church and long row of seventeenth century Weavers' cottages. It's split in two by the River Coln, which adds a lovely picnic and duck-feeding spot to the village's charm. Predictably, Bibury can also boast at least one coachload of tourists. Don't worry – the ride carries you out onto a good loop through the surrounding countryside and villages. The riding is enjoyable and never demanding, featuring open tracks, fast descents and gentle climbs. A great way to explore a lovely area of the country.

The Ride

Leave the tourists behind by heading east out of Bibury and following lanes through open countryside to the small but attractive village of Coln St Aldwyns. Pick up the dead-straight line of Akeman Street – once a major Roman Road linking London to Cirencester – and follow quiet lanes to the most easterly point of the ride. Swap tarmac for grass and follow field edges and then good tracks back west. The odd easy climb and descent adds interest as you climb to the highpoint of the route at Saltway Farm, from where a gradual descent on easy tracks drops towards Ablington. Splash through an ever-present, cow-infested puddle and follow quiet lanes past the trout farm to Bibury.

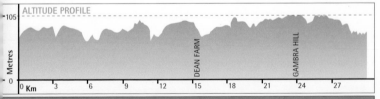

BIBURY   GRADE: ▲

TOTAL DISTANCE: 30KM » **TOTAL ASCENT**: 280M » **TIME**: 2–4 HOURS » **START/FINISH**: THE SWAN HOTEL IN BIBURY
START GRID REF: SP 114068 » **SATNAV**: GL7 5NW » **PARKING**: ON-STREET IN BIBURY » **OS MAP**: LANDRANGER 163
PUB: THE CATHERINE WHEEL, BIBURY, TEL: 01285 740 250 » **CAFÉ**: THERE'S A CAFE IN THE TROUT FARM

08 **BIBURY**

Directions – Bibury

⑨ With your back to the Swan Hotel, turn **L** and take the main road alongside the river and out of Bibury. Keep **R** at the fork. At the T-junction, turn **R** to Coln St Aldwyns.

2 Once in the village, turn **L** at the junction and ride into the village of Hatherop. Turn **L** at the junction. Follow the road for 3.5km before turning **L** immediately after a small cottage, on to a grassy bridleway. Head into the field and bear **R** to a narrow gate. Go through this and drop to the road. Turn **L**.

3 After 600m, turn **L**, following bridleway signs up a grassy track. Follow this to a track junction and go **SA** past the barn. Keep **SA** onto a grassy track after 350m and follow this through a gate and in front of the woods to a track T-junction. Turn **R** and follow doubletrack to the lane.

4 Go **SA** up the lane and turn **L** onto a signed bridleway as the road bends sharply right. Follow the bridleway to a T-junction with a wide track and turn **L**, dropping to the farm. Ride through the farm and up the lane for 200m before turning **R** onto a signed bridleway. Turn **R** in front of the woods and then turn **L** up their far side.

5 At the road, go **SA** onto a narrow lane. Go **SA** over the crossroads and, after 1km turn **L** on to a signed bridleway just after a small set of woods. Follow this past a large metal barn to a track crossroads with a gate ahead of you.

Optional Route – Short Cut

OR Go **SA** through the gate and ignore all turnings until you reach a concrete lane. Follow this to the road and turn **R** to the centre of Bibury.

6 Turn **R** and follow the track. Kink to the left and then right as you meet a hedge blocking your way and follow the track to the road.

7 Keep **SA** and, after just over 1km, turn **L** onto a wide track, signed as a public byway just before a house. Follow this, ignoring turnings, to the road. Turn **L** and then immediately **L** again on to another wide track. Splash through the big puddle, keep **R** near the barn and continue into the village of Ablington. Bear **L** at the first T-junction and **R** at the next, to follow the road back to Bibury.

09 Guiting Power

28km

Introduction

Good riding, a decent distance and a fair amount of climbing – a solid ride. There's plenty going on: bridleways through grassy fields, easy stretches of hard-packed track and fast descents over loose surfaces. Best of all is the bridleway running east from Aston Farm. Beginning in the woods, it moves steadily through the trees before crossing a field and sweeping down flowing singletrack into a low valley. There is a fair amount of road, but as always with the Cotswolds, the surroundings are picturesque and the villages are pleasant, so it's far from a bad situation! Speaking of villages, Guiting Power and Upper Slaughter are unbelievably twee and well worth a quick look as you pass through – there's even an optional extension to the route if you want to visit Lower Slaughter and feed the ducks...

The Ride

Gain height easily on the road climb out of the awesomely-named Guiting Power and catch your breath on the grassy bridleways that follow. Drop fast through fields and then take a wide track alongside the river into Upper Slaughter. An easy climb on a narrow stony track and a short, but enjoyable, descent lead to the highlight of the ride: muddy singletrack through the woods behind Aston Farm and the singletrack swoop into the valley beyond. It's a shame it's not longer! Plod along the base of the pretty valley, say 'Hello!' to the horses and then grit your teeth for the steep pull out. This time, be glad it's not longer! Another fun, but diminutive descent drops into Naunton, from where quiet lanes and wide tracks carry you home via fast descents and quiet stretches of road.

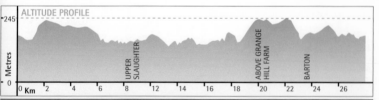

GUITING POWER   **GRADE:** ▲

TOTAL DISTANCE: 28KM » **TOTAL ASCENT**: 550M » **TIME**: 2–4 HOURS » **START/FINISH**: VILLAGE GREEN, GUITING POWER
START GRID REF: SP 094247 » **SATNAV**: GUITING POWER » **PARKING**: PAY AND DISPLAY, GUITING POWER
OS MAP: LANDRANGER 163 » **PUB**: HOLLOW BOTTOM, GUITING POWER, TEL: 01451 850 392; FARMER'S ARMS, GUITING
POWER, 01451 850 358 » **CAFÉ**: SMALL CAFE IN THE POST OFFICE IN GUITING POWER

09 GUITING POWER

Directions – Guiting Power

❻ With your back to the village green on the main road in the centre of Guiting Power, turn **R** and ride out of the village. Turn **R** at the T-junction and then take the next **L**.

2 Turn **R** at the next junction, following signs for *Naunton*. Take the fourth **R**, after approximately 2.5km, and immediately turn **L** through a gate onto a grassy bridleway. Follow this, parallel to the road, through gates and across a farm entrance lane.

3 At the end of the bridleway, go **SA** across the main road and through a gate onto a wide track. Follow this past a barn, through gates and across fields. At the main road, turn **L** and then turn **R** onto a wide, signed bridleway opposite the house. At the road, keep **R** and climb above the river and ford (optional water splash, but beware it's a slippery one!). Keep **R** at the triangular junction and turn **L** at the T-junction.

Optional Route – For Lower Slaughter and feeding the ducks...
OR Turn **L** after 300m and follow the road into Lower Slaughter. Turn **R** onto a signed bridleway on a bend in the river opposite the 'Lower Slaughter Manor Restaurant and Hotel' (looks like a footpath). Bear **R** after the gate and turn **R** at the road. After a short way, turn **L** up a bridleway opposite a road turning and pick up the directions just after **4**).

4 After 1km, turn **R** onto a signed bridleway opposite a road turning. Go **SA** over the road into a field and bear diagonally **R**. Turn **L** after the gate and drop to a track T-junction. Turn **R** and go **SA** for a short distance up the road before turning **R** into Aston Farm (signed).

5 Go through the farm and follow vague tracks across the field beyond. Go into the woods and follow wide singletrack, ignoring turnings. Cross a field and turn **L** after the gate on the far side. Follow singletrack down into the valley and keep **SA** along a vague grassy track along the valley floor.

6 Go **SA** over the road onto more vague tracks through gates and fields. After crossing a small stone bridge, climb steeply up the obvious track. Pass the golf course and go **SA** across the road. Go through a gate and drop down singletrack and a wider track to the road. Turn **R** at the T-junction, cross the river and turn **L**. Climb out of the village and go **SA** over the road T-junction onto a dirt track by the quarry.

7 At the road, turn **R** and then, after a short distance, **L** onto a wide track. Follow this to the road and turn **R**. Follow the road into Temple Guiting and turn **L** upon passing the Temple Guiting signs. When the road swings sharp right, turn **L** onto a wide track. At the road, turn **R**.

8 Drop downhill and cross the river. Climb through a gate and turn **L** on a dirt track past a small car park. At the T-junction, turn **L** and drop downhill, keeping **R** at the bottom of the short descent. Follow the track to a lane, ride this to a T-junction and turn **L** into the centre of Guiting Power.

10 Castle Combe

Introduction

Set to the south of the M4, away from the main body of the Cotswolds, this is a subtly different ride. Passing close to the Castle Combe race circuit, on the right/wrong day, you can hear the cars roaring around. So, although the usual quaint villages and 'old England' scenery are present and correct, you shouldn't expect peace and quiet! (A few years ago the circuit had to cut noise levels – imagine what it used to sound like!) The riding also seems to differ slightly around here. The bridleways are a touch narrower and there's a little more (legal) singletrack than you'll find further north. The descents are just right for less-experienced riders to scoot down, while faster riders can barrel through with equal enjoyment. There is a degree of road riding along the way, but it's more than made up for by the technical sections.

The Ride

The ride begins with a stretch along the road. Luckily, the usual Cotswolds Charm™ rule applies and you barely notice it. Failing that, the roar of racetrack engines is something of a distraction! Easy, but pleasant byways lead to the first stretch of more exciting riding – a short, but disconcertingly loose slide to Castle Combe. Riding through the pretty village, it's obvious why the tourists come here! A fast woodland descent, a singletrack climb and then quiet roads lead to a technical singletrack drop into the woods beyond North Wraxall. This is great – easy enough to be fast, technical enough to keep you awake! The next highlight is another descent – a narrow, wet and rocky jaw-clencher to Widdenham Farm and onto a fast stretch of singletrack. Another climb sets you up for the final descent. This is a much wider affair, with higher speeds and big grins to match. A final climb, and you're back in Biddestone.

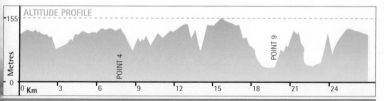

CASTLE COMBE GRADE: ▲

TOTAL DISTANCE: 27KM » **TOTAL ASCENT**: 600M » **TIME**: 2–4 HOURS » **START/FINISH**: BIDDESTONE VILLAGE POND
START GRID REF: ST 863734 » **SATNAV**: SN14 7DG » **PARKING**: ON-STREET IN BIDDESTONE » **OS MAP**: LANDRANGER 173
PUB: THE WHITE HORSE, BIDDESTONE, TEL: 01249 713 305; BIDDESTONE ARMS, BIDDESTONE, TEL: 01249 714 377

10 CASTLE COMBE

Directions – Castle Combe

➏ With your back to the village green, turn **L** along the main road through Biddestone. Fork **L** after 350m and head out of the village.

2 Ignoring all turnings, ride to the main road. Hop over the kerb, carefully cross the road and go **SA** down the lane. Once again, ignore turnings until the road drops downhill and swings right. Turn **R** at this point through a gate onto a marked bridleway. Keep **L** on the obvious track and ride up the valley. Pass through gates and follow bridleway signs before joining tarmac briefly in front of a house. Continue **SA** across the small field beyond and go through a gate to the road. Don't worry if you hear a lot of engine noise – it's probably not traffic...

3 Turn **L**, pass an entrance to Castle Combe Circuit and turn **R** on to a wide, signed byway. At the road, go **SA** for a short distance and then keep **SA** onto a second byway.

4 At the road, turn **L**. Turn **L** at the T-junction, follow the main road to a big left-hand bend and turn **R** off the main road. Immediately turn **R** again onto a narrow lane. After 200m, turn **R** onto a bridleway and drop through the woods.

5 At the road, turn **L** into Castle Combe. Follow the road through the village and climb to a T-junction. Go **SA** over the road, through a gate and turn **R**, following bridleway signs. Descend rapidly to the river, go through the gate and climb the obvious track to a house. Pass through what appears to be the back garden and turn **R** along the wide track. Continue **SA** onto the road and turn **L** at the T-junction. Descend to North Wraxall.

6 Turn **L** at the T-junction, drop through the houses and climb steeply through the village. Turn **R** onto a narrow bridleway and climb steeply to the main road. Cross carefully and go **SA** down a narrow lane.

7 At the end of the lane, fork **R** onto the right-hand singletrack and drop into the woods. Cross the stream and bear **R**. Climb, ignoring all turnings, until the gradient eases and you reach a (flat) T-junction. Turn **L**.

8 Follow the obvious track around to the right and then fork **R** up and out of the trees. Go **SA** along field edges to the road. Go **SA** and then, after 700m, turn **L**. Go **SA** at the next crossroads, onto a narrow dead-end lane. Drop downhill through a rather fancy gate and turn **L** through a second gate onto a wide track as the lane bends right. Follow for about 500m and then turn **L** through a third gate. Follow grassy tracks downhill to a good track. After a short distance, bear **L** onto a short section of steep singletrack. At the road, turn **R**.

Optional Route – Short Cut

OR Or, to take 4km off the length of the ride (and miss a descent), instead turn **L** through the gate into a field. Pick up the directions at **11**).

9 As the road bends right by a farm, go **SA** through the gate into a field. Go **SA** across the field to a second gate, and then bear **R** across the next field to the road.

10 Turn **L** and climb steeply before turning **L** onto a signed bridleway. Climb singletrack to the road and continue **SA**. Turn **L** at the T-junction and, just after the houses, turn **L** onto a track signed *Unsuitable for Vehicles*. Keep **SA** at the junction and then bear **R** onto narrow singletrack. Keep **SA** on the lane through the farm to a sharp left-hand bend and then turn **R** through a gate into the field.

11 Follow obvious tracks across the field and through the gate onto singletrack. At the farm track, turn **R** and climb to the woods. Once in the woods, take the second **L** (the only turning that isn't gated with a *Private* sign) and descend rapidly.

12 Climb out of the woods and continue **SA**, ignoring turnings, to Biddestone.

11 Naunton

34km

Introduction

A couple of cheeky little descents (if only they were longer!), a few short climbs and some easy cruising through the countryside make up this enjoyable ride. There's nothing hard, although the descent to Broadwater Bottom is disconcertingly steep and bumpy (let off the brakes!) and the short stretch of singletrack east of Aston Farm is, as I've harped on about on the other rides that use it, rather good. Hopping between villages in the central Cotswolds, you're never far from houses, although only Cold Aston and the start/finish village of Naunton have pubs – something to bear in mind if you want some refreshment halfway round.

The Ride

Get up out of the saddle, pick a big gear and stomp your way up the road climb out of Naunton. Carry your speed through the next couple of road descents to make the following climbs easier and then sit back and spin into Notgrove in the big ring. Grind up the grassy field, zip through the woods leading to Cold Aston and then blast along the wide, easy tracks running south-east to Hazelton. Cruise along field edges and a short section of singletrack, whizz along the road and enjoy the views from the ridge behind Leygore Manor. Stay off the brakes on the short, but bumpy and mildly-terrifying descent to Broadwater Bottom and head north to Aston Farm. Head through the woods and grin as you fly down the singletrack on the far side. Chill out along the valley bottom, ignore the burn in your legs on the climb and nip down the short descent back to Naunton.

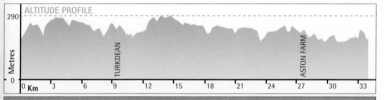

ALTITUDE PROFILE

290

Metres

0

| 0 Km | 3 | 6 | 9 TURKDEAN | 12 | 15 | 18 | 21 | 24 | 27 ASTON FARM | 30 | 33 |

NAUNTON

GRADE: ▲

TOTAL DISTANCE: 34KM » **TOTAL ASCENT**: 650M » **TIME**: 2.5–5 HOURS » **START/FINISH**: VILLAGE GREEN IN NAUNTON
START GRID REF: SP 113234 » **SATNAV**: NAUNTON » **PARKING**: ON-STREET IN NAUNTON » **OS MAP**: LANDRANGER 163
PUB: BLACK HORSE, NAUNTON, TEL: 01451 850 565; THE PLOUGH, COLD ASTON, TEL: 01451 821 459 » **CAFÉ**: PICNIC TIME!

11 NAUNTON

❺ With your back to the small triangular green (near the church) in Naunton, turn **R** and follow the main road through the village. Climb to the road junction and go **SA**, following signs for Notgrove. Continue **SA** over the next road junction, still signed *Notgrove*, and follow the road to the right. Turn **L** just after a large metal barn and drop to the village. Turn **L** onto a narrow lane as you reach the grassy area. Tackle a short climb and then turn **L**, following bridleway signs through a metal gate.

2 Cross the field ahead and climb to a gate on the far side. Go through this and turn **R** along the wide track. As you reach the trees, turn **L**, still following bridleway signs, and follow the bridleway up through the narrow strip of woodland. At the road, turn **R** and ride into Cold Aston. Take the first **R** and follow the lane through the farm onto a dirt track. Follow this, ignoring all turnings, to the road.

3 At the T-junction, turn **R**. Almost immediately, turn **L** to pass through the farm to a gate onto a wide track. Follow this track into and along the valley to two gates. Go through the left-hand gate and climb gradually to the village of Hazleton. Follow the road through the village and turn **L** onto a wide track immediately in front of a large metal barn. Continue **SA** onto grass as the track bends left and turn **R** at the T-junction with a narrow bridleway. Follow singletrack to the road.

4 Taking care – this is a busy road – turn **L** and then **R**, signed *Compton Abdale*. Follow the lane, keeping **L** at the fork, before turning **L** through wide metal gates onto a signed bridleway.

5 Drop to a track junction and turn **R** onto a concrete track. Follow this to the road and turn **R**. Almost immediately, turn **L** and follow bridleway signs onto an obvious track passing to the right of the barn. Cross the field and then turn **R** along the hedge and field edge. Go through the gate and turn **L**. Taking care – this is a busy junction – go **SA** over the roundabout and turn **L** onto a minor road signed *Turkdean*. Drop and climb out of a dip and then turn **R** onto a wide track leading to Leygore Manor. Pass to the left of the house and into the field. Continue **SA** until you reach the hedge and turn **R** off the track and through a gate to the road.

6 Turn **L** (again, watch out for traffic) for 700m and then turn **L** onto a narrow bridleway. Drop down the bumpy track. Go **SA** into the field and take the obvious track up the slope ahead.

7 Ride into Cold Aston and turn **L** at the T-junction. Turn **R** in front of the pub and ride out of the village towards Bourton. Turn **L** at the junction with the A436 and, after 400m, turn **R** onto a minor road. Drop downhill and turn **L** into Aston Farm (signed).

8 Go through the farm and follow vague tracks across the field beyond. Go into the woods and follow wide singletrack, ignoring turnings. Cross a field and turn **L** after the gate on the far side. Follow singletrack down into the valley and keep **SA** along a vague grassy track along the valley floor.

9 Go **SA** over the road onto more vague tracks through gates and fields. After crossing a small stone bridge, climb steeply up the obvious track. Pass the golf course and go **SA** across the road. Go through a gate and drop down singletrack and a wider track to Naunton.

12 Nailsworth

Introduction

Beginning with a steep road climb and then following easy tracks, this route ends with one of the best descents in the Cotswolds. Or at least, one of my favourites. It's not an overly technical ride, although the final descent can get a bit sketchy if taken at speed in the wet. On that note, the ride does hold up reasonably well in winter, as many of the tracks are stone-based. Talking of stones, the final descent has multiple lines in places, some of which rattle fast over rocks. Compared to many of the other routes in the guide, this ride doesn't offer expansive views – although the surroundings are pleasant – as many of the tracks are in the trees. This is particularly true of the final descent, which drops steeply through woodland, sliding over roots and dodging branches. So, a fun route with some good riding and a now massively over-hyped final descent...

The Ride

Unfortunately, this ride doesn't begin with a spot of road riding. It begins with a right old uphill slog on the road. Don't worry – it's height saved for later. A bit of loose bridleway and a quick road spin later, the route joins the Macmillan Way. This is a fast byway that narrows to singletrack in places and carries you south for a good five and a half kilometres. Easy tracks and a couple of short rocky tests lead to the hillside above Avening. Pretend you're a road rider and zoom down to the village in an aero tuck before sitting up to climb back out. A fast grassy descent and a quiet lane now set you up for the highlight of the ride – the drop back in to Nailsworth. This is a fast, muddy and rooty plummet through the woods, with multiple line choices and either a rocky, or twisting finale.

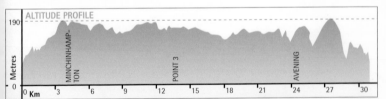

NAILSWORTH   **GRADE:** ▲

TOTAL DISTANCE: 30KM » **TOTAL ASCENT**: 550M » **TIME**: 2–4 HOURS » **START/FINISH**: NAILSWORTH CLOCK TOWER
START GRID REF: ST 850997 » **SATNAV**: NAILSWORTH » **PARKING**: PLENTY OF CAR PARKS IN NAILSWORTH
OS MAP: LANDRANGER 162 & 163 » **PUB**: LOTS OF CHOICE » **CAFÉ**: LOTS OF CHOICE

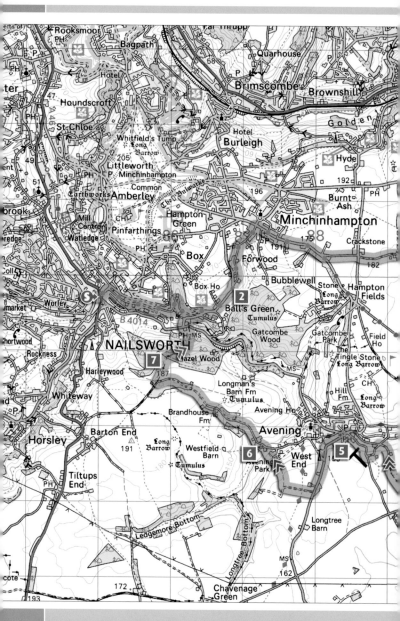

12 NAILSWORTH

➏ Take George Street – the road to the right of the clock tower, signed to *Minchinhampton* – for 100m, passing a car park on your right and then turn **R** onto a very narrow minor road. Follow this for 1.5km to a T-junction and turn **L**.

2 Ride uphill to a fork and bear **R**. Climb steeply into Minchinhampton and turn **R** at the crossroads. Follow the road out of the houses, bearing **L** at the fork. Go **SA** at the crossroads and continue **SA** onto the wide track as the road ends. Keep going **SA**, ignoring all turnings, passing through trees and alongside the airfield and then follow vague tracks as they bear **R** across a grassy field to a gate and the road. Turn **L**, keep **L** at the fork and go **SA** at the crossroads.

3 Go **SA** over the main road and, after 1.25km, turn **R** onto a wide track. Go **SA** (slightly **R**) over the first road, **SA** onto and off the second road and then **SA** over the third. At the fourth road, turn **R** and then almost immediately **L**. At the T-junction, go **SA** onto a signed bridleway.

4 At the road, keep **SA** onto a lane. After 600m, turn **R** onto a rutted track. Follow this down a short rocky section and then, upon meeting tarmac, immediately turn **L** and climb a rocky track to the road.

5 Turn **R** and drop into the outskirts of Avening. Take the first **L** as you enter the village (the main road, signed *Tetbury*) and climb away from the houses. After 1km, turn **R** onto a dirt lane. As the lane swings to the left at the trees, turn **R** onto a wide track. Follow along the field edge, through the trees, and drop fast through a gate and out to the lane.

6 Turn **L** and follow the lane to a farm. Continue onto a wide, loose track and ride into the woods. As the track bends sharply left on the far side of the woods, turn **R**, following bridleway signs. Ride along the field edge and go **SA** at the bridleway junction.

7 Make your way down the brilliant descent that follows via shallow gullies and across fields. At the road, turn **L** and then **R** opposite the pub. Climb steeply uphill before turning **L** and retracing your steps to the clock tower.

SECTION 3

Enduros

*Warmed up? Enduros are rides that
make the most of a day out in the hills.
Make sure you've got your multi-tool,
some lunch and some willing legs.
These are challenging rides for fit
and experienced riders and want to
feel the burn.*

Enduros
sponsored by GORE
BIKE WEAR™
www.gorebikewear.com

NEAR CHAVENAGE GREEN (ROUTE 13)

CLASSIC COTSWOLDS TERRAIN NEAR UPPER COSCOMBE (ROUTE 15)

13 Crudwell Classic

44km

Introduction

This is one of those rides where you get the bike up to speed and relax, pedalling happily away as the countryside whizzes past. I first rode a route very similar to this in a local Trailquest event (essentially orienteering on bikes – www.midlandtrailquests.co.uk if you fancy a go). Whilst we'd probably have scored more points looping anti-clockwise, we figured the riding was more fun this way round. Anyway, back to the point – whilst this is a fairly long ride, there are only a couple of technically difficult sections and very little climbing, considering the distance covered. This makes the route a great choice if you want a long, straightforward ride through some beautiful countryside. It's worth noting that a couple of sections of the route (generally the more technical ones) do get pretty sticky in the winter – check the alternative routes on the map – although the rest is fine whatever the weather.

The Ride

The first dirt encountered on the ride is the wide Fosse Way. This, like the Macmillan Way that's joined 5km later, is well surfaced and easy to ride, and the two byways carry you quickly north. Turning west on roads and grassy trails, the route passes the airfield near Minchinhampton and dives on to the first real descent of the ride – a fast, gravelly blast down to Avening. Dirt tracks lead away from the village in to the woods – look alongside the track and you'll spot sections of narrow trail used on motorbike rallies. The route now heads south, switching between singletrack, bumpy trails and wide tracks. There's a short, root-infested descent on the way out of Chavenage Green, and another further south, just before Shipton Moyne. From here, the return to leg to Crudwell begins on the Fosse Way. Wider and faster here, the byway swoops through a deep ford as it straight-lines its way home.

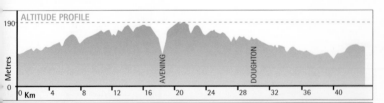

ALTITUDE PROFILE

190

Metres

0

| 0 Km | 4 | 8 | 12 | 16 | 20 | 24 | 28 | 32 | 36 | 40 |

AVENING

DOUGHTON

CRUDWELL CLASSIC

GRADE: ▲

TOTAL DISTANCE: 44KM » **TOTAL ASCENT**: 450M » **TIME**: 3•5 HOURS » **START/FINISH**: TRIANGULAR VILLAGE GREEN IN CRUDWELL
START GRID REF: ST 955929 » **SATNAV**: GL7 2LB » **PARKING**: ON-STREET IN CRUDWELL » **OS MAP**: LANDRANGERS 162, 163 & 173
PUB: THE PLOUGH INN, CRUDWELL, TEL: 01666 577 833; THE WHEATSHEAF, CRUDWELL, TEL: 01666 577 739; THE BELL, AVENING, TEL: 01453 836 422 » **CAFÉ**: BRING SANDWICHES

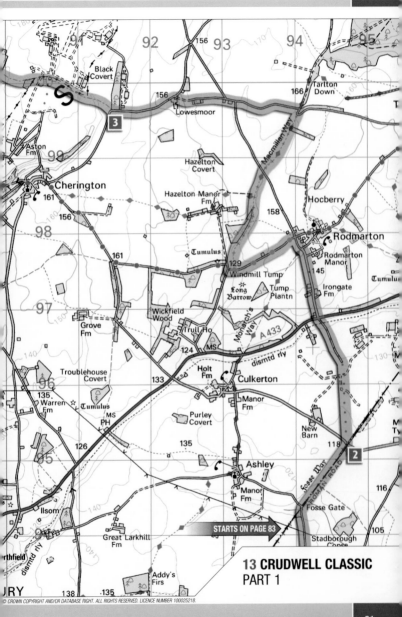

13 CRUDWELL CLASSIC
PART 1

STARTS ON PAGE 83

13 CRUDWELL CLASSIC
PART 2

Directions – Crudwell Classic

➲ From the triangular green in Crudwell, head south, towards Malmesbury and the M4. After 400m, turn **R** onto Tetbury Lane, towards the village hall. Ride out of the houses and turn **R** at the first junction. After 1.75km, turn **R** onto the wide, signposted *Fosse Way*.

2 At the road, cross over and bear **L** through a gate into a field. Cross the field to a wide track, turn **L**, follow this around to the **R** and then turn **L** onto a grassy bridleway in front of the hedge and go through a gate. At the road, go **SA** towards Rodmarton and turn **L** at the crossroads. Drop gently downhill for 1km and then turn **R** onto an unsigned dirt track (Macmillan Way) immediately before the road junction. Go **SA** at the first road and then turn **L** at the second. Ignore the first left turn and then bear **L** at the fork. At the T-junction, turn **L**.

3 As the road bends left, turn **R** through a gate into a field. Cross the field and go **SA**, ignoring all turnings, alongside the airfield. Go through the woods and follow the wide track out past houses. At the crossroads, turn **L**. Go **SA** over the crossroads in Hampton Fields and turn **L** (virtually **SA**) at the T-junction. After a short distance, fork **R** onto a wide stony track and drop into Avening. Turn **R** at the road junction and drop to the main road.

4 Turn **R** and then turn **L** up the last road you reach before leaving the houses. Keep **R** as the road forks and then bear **L** onto the narrower of the two bridleways as the road ends.

Optional Route – Wet weather option
▶ Instead, turn **L** at the main road, and then **R** in front of the pub. Ignoring all turnings, follow the lane for 2km and bear **R** through the farm on to a wide track. Rejoin the directions at **5**.

5 Keep **SA** onto a wide track as you enter the woods. Follow this out of the woods, keeping **R** at the first fork and **L** at the second. Drop to the road and turn **L** to climb steeply for 1km. Turn **L** onto a wide track directly opposite the petrol station and follow the bridleway, through gates, to a track crossroads and go **SA**.

6   Upon meeting a wide track, turn **R** and ride to the road. Turn **L**. After 700m, turn **R** as you approach the houses and ride through the farmyard. Bear **L**, following bridleway signs and obvious tracks to descend through trees. Climb steeply **SA** up the field ahead.

7   At the road, turn **R** and then almost immediately **L** onto a wide track. Follow this to the road and turn **R**, then almost immediately **L**. Follow the lane to a crossroads, turn **L** and then go carefully **SA** over the main road.

8   After a short distance, turn **L** and pass through a small and very tidy farmyard onto a bridleway. Follow this to the road and turn **R**. After 200m, turn **R** again onto a bridleway, leading to a short technical descent to the stream. Go **SA** up the steep bank ahead and turn **R** at the T-junction. At the road turn **L**.

Optional Route – Wet weather option

▶OR▷   Instead, keep **SA** along the lane and keep **L** at the junction. Follow the lane into Shipton Moyne and pick up the directions at **9**.

9   At the crossroads, turn **R** and ride through Shipton Moyne. As the road bends left, continue **SA** onto a very wide, well-surfaced track. Follow this to a track T-junction and turn **L** onto the Fosse Way. Go **SA** over the road, still on the Fosse Way and then **SA** onto a lane as the dirt track ends. As the lane bends sharply right, keep **SA**, moving back onto dirt once more. Drop downhill, tackle the ford and then continue **SA** across two roads. At the third, turn **R** and ride back into Crudwell, retracing your steps to the start point.

14 Birdlip

29km

Introduction

Following good trails through lovely scenery, this relatively lengthy route is a worthwhile choice if you're looking for a less technical day out. Although the riding isn't difficult, there are a few memorable descents to put a smile on your face. There's the dirt descent from Elkstone, the sweeping drop towards the River Churn and the fast, loose tracks from Upper Coberley and Leckhampton Hill. To balance things out, there are also a few climbs to contend with – ranging from steep grassy pulls to the stony, traction-spitting trail towards the radio masts on Shab Hill – you'll need strong legs! The rest of the ride runs along easy trails, passing through pleasant valleys, across open fields and through some lovely woods. The best view, however, comes at the start and finish of the ride at Birdlip viewpoint, stretching out towards Gloucester.

The Ride

Leaving the viewpoint, a quick road warm up leads into Witcombe Wood, from where an enjoyable stretch of singletrack and a pleasant field edge cruise run to Brimpsfield Park. Grab a handful of low gears and dig deep as you clamber uphill towards the A417. Duck under this, follow more field edges and then drop fast into a green and pleasant valley south east of Elkstone. After you've scrambled out of this, a fast, grassy swoop drops to Colesbourne and a long, shallow track climbs away past a cottage hidden deep in the woods. Hit the road briefly and then rattle down a fast farm track descent. Another spot of road work and another fast descent set you up for the tricky climb onto Shab Hill. Descend rapidly into Coldwell Bottom, grind out of the other side and cruise easily home.

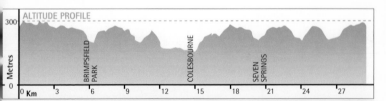

ALTITUDE PROFILE

300

Metres

0

0 Km   3   6   9   12   15   18   21   24   27

BRIMPSFIELD PARK

COLESBOURNE

SEVEN SPRINGS

BIRDLIP **GRADE:** ▲

TOTAL DISTANCE: 29KM » **TOTAL ASCENT**: 600M » **TIME**: 2.5–5 HOURS » **START/FINISH**: BIRDLIP VIEWPOINT CAR PARK **START GRID REF**: SO 931153 » **SATNAV**: BIRDLIP » **PARKING**: BIRDLIP VIEWPOINT CAR PARK » **OS MAP**: LANDRANGER 163 **PUB**: AIR BALLOON, ON THE A417, TEL: 01452 862 541; ROYAL GEORGE HOTEL, BIRDLIP, TEL: 01452 862 506

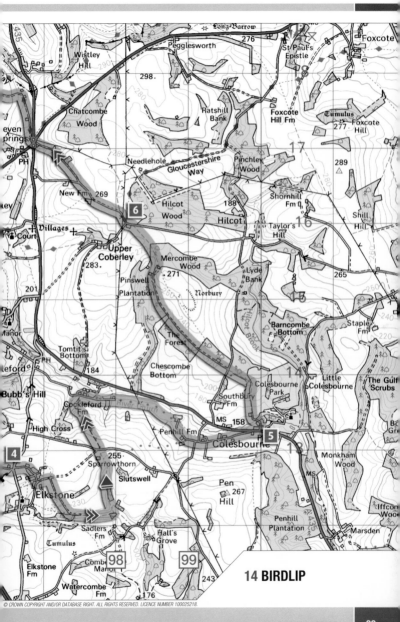

14 BIRDLIP

Directions — Birdlip

➏ Leave the car park, and go **SA** up the road. At the T-junction, turn **R** to Birdlip. Follow the road around a right-hand bend and then turn **L**, following signs for Stroud.

2 After 800m, turn **L** onto a vague but signed bridleway running into the woods. Head through the trees and turn **L** at the track T-junction on the far side of the woods. Follow obvious singletrack to the road and turn **R**. Immediately after the house, turn **L** onto a signed bridleway. At the road, turn **R**.

3 Go **SA** where the road bends sharply left. Go past the houses and around the edge of the field. At the road, turn **L**. At the T-junction, turn **R** and then almost immediately **L** onto a tarmac lane, signed *Brimpsfield Park*. Bear **R** at the farm onto a good track and drop into a valley. Keep following the track to climb steeply through fields. At the dual carriageway, turn **L** through a gate and take the tunnel under the road. Follow tarmac up to a gate and turn **L**, across fields. At the road, turn **R**.

4 Go **SA** over the crossroads and follow the road through the village. As the houses on the left give way to open ground, turn **L** onto a wide track signed as a public path. As you enter fields, turn **R** and follow muddy tracks into a pleasant valley. Turn **L** at the bottom, following bridleway signs to climb, initially on grassy tracks into woods and through to the road. Go **SA** over the road, through a gate and onto vague grassy tracks. Trending slightly **L**, descend on increasingly obvious tracks. At the lane, turn **R** and continue **SA** as tarmac ends, along grassy tracks. At the house, follow the gravel track and lane out to the road junction. Turn **L** and ride to the main road. Turn **R** to Colesbourne.

5 Turn **L** onto a lane immediately after the pub. Go **SA** at the end of the lane, onto grass. At the gate, move **R** and climb alongside the woods. Follow the track through the woods to the road. Go **SA** onto a very obvious track. Ignoring all turnings, follow this for just over 1.5km. Keep **R** at the fork, go past an awesome little cottage and turn **L** at the singletrack T-junction in the woods. Ride out across fields to the road and turn **L**.

6   Keep **R** at the junction. After 800m, turn **R** onto a wide track as the road bends left. Drop to the main road. Turn **R**, and take the first exit off the roundabout onto a minor lane with *Gates* signs. Follow the lane for 2km, pass a white house on the right and turn **L** onto a wide track. Follow this, ignoring turnings, to the road. Turn **L**.

7   At the main road, go **SA** and then bear **R** onto a stony track. Follow this until you meet tarmac and turn **L**. Continue **SA** as tarmac ends and follow tracks downhill, looking out for a gate on the **R** by a metal bridleway signpost. Go through this and drop into the valley. At the bottom, cross the valley floor and climb on grassy tracks diagonally up the other side to a gate. Go through this and immediately turn **R**.

8   Go through a small gate on the **L** as the track ends, but continue **SA** to fields. Keep going **SA** across the field to buildings. Go between these to a tarmac lane. Turn **L** and follow this back to the car park.

15 Snowshill

Introduction

If you were a crow, and you happened to fly east across the north Cotswolds, you'd hit a big hill half way across. This hill provides the basis for this ride, which flits up and down the side via a couple of great descents and tough climbs. The first descent, at the southern end of the ride, is a flat-out rocky blast, while the second and third are narrower, muddier affairs. All three will have you squawking with delight! A technical route with a decent amount of climbing, this is one of the harder rides in the area and you'll need to be a fairly fit and confident rider to get the most from it. Once you've finished, visit Snowshill Manor and its impressive gardens and collections of Samurai armour and bicycles. The churchyard opposite has a war memorial and there's a lavender farm (ever seen one of them before?) just outside the village.

The Ride

The ride starts innocently enough, cruising through the picturesque village of Snowshill, across fields and along quiet lanes. It soon moves on to dirt tracks, which become narrower and more entertaining as you travel south, before launching down a fast, rock-strewn descent. The ride then winches its way back up the hill via the first of the route's big climbs. This isn't technical, but it is steep. The second descent of the route follows quickly. This is a fast grassy affair with a rocky sting in its tail... A tough climb up an energy-sapping track sees you back up in Snowshill. You could finish your ride here, or you could tackle the steep road climb out of the village, safe in the knowledge that it's leading to an entertaining singletrack descent that spits you out just below the car park.

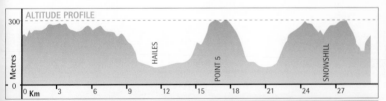

SNOWSHILL   **GRADE:** ▲

TOTAL DISTANCE: 30KM » **TOTAL ASCENT**: 750M » **TIME**: 2.5–5 HOURS » **START/FINISH**: FREE CAR PARK NORTH OF SNOWSHILL
START GRID REF: SP 096342 » **SATNAV**: WR12 7JU » **OS MAP**: LANDRANGER 150 & 163 » **PUB**: SNOWSHILL ARMS,
SNOWSHILL, TEL: 01386 852 653; MOUNT INN, STANTON, TEL: 01386 584 316 » **CAFÉ**: PICNIC TIME!

15 SNOWSHILL

Directions – Snowshill

⑤➜ Turn **R** out of the car park and follow the road through Snowshill. Climb out of the village and take the first **R** down a dead end lane. Keep **L** at the fork and, after 100m, turn **L** onto a farm access lane. Pass to the right-hand side of the farm onto a grassy bridleway and follow this to the road.

2 Turn sharp **R** onto the right-hand of the two lanes (parallel to the wood) and keep **SA** at the junction. At the T-junction with the main road, go **SA** onto a wide track. Follow this into the trees and then continue **SA** through a gate as the main track bends left.

3 At the road, turn **R**. As the lane ends, continue **SA** onto a wide track and rattle down a rocky descent. Continue **SA** onto the road and turn **R** at the junction. At the main road, turn **R** and then immediately **R** again, towards Didbrook. Follow the road to a crossroads with the B4077.

4 **Take care** – this can be busy. Turn **R**, signed *Stow*. After 1km, bear **L** off the main road at a group of houses. Go **SA** between buildings onto a narrow bridleway marked *No Motor Vehicles*. Follow the bridleway to a multi-track junction near a stone hut. Turn **R**, (the third track, counting rightwards from the hut) climbing the obvious wide track. Keep **R** (in effect **SA**) at the next junction, climb, and bear **L** to leave the woods near a stone barn.

5 As the woods end, bear **L** through a gate and follow the bridleway across fields. Pass through another two gates, turning sharp **L** immediately after the second gate (third gate in total) through a double gate and follow the low stone wall to a farm. Turn **R**, pass through the farm and turn **R** after the cattle grid. Follow this to the road and turn **L** onto an obvious track (**not** straight ahead – you're coming back up here later). Pass through a gate and drop to the village of Stanton. Follow the main road through the village, turning **R** at the T-junction.

6 At the main road, turn **R** and take the first **R**, towards Laverton. Go through the village to a wide byway. Climb this to a T-junction and turn **R** on a good track.

7 Follow the track on to tarmac. Turn **L** along the lane and ride into Snowshill. Turn **R** just before the church. Climb through the village, go **SA** over the first crossroads and turn **L** at the second, following signs for Snowshill Lavender.

8 Immediately after the sawmill, turn **L** onto a narrow bridleway (**easy to miss**). Follow this across fields and through a gate into the woods. Keep close to the edge of the woods on a wide track. As this track bends right, continue **SA** onto singletrack. Follow this until it swings to the right and drops to fields. Go **SA** across the fields, following bridleway signs (**easy to miss**) to the road. Turn **L** and climb to the car park.

SNOWSHILL LAVENDER

16 Bisley

Introduction

This isn't a nice, tidy 'loop'. It criss-crosses the map, retraces its steps and makes U-turns here and there, giving it a somewhat contrived air. However, there's a good, rather loose and rocky reason for this: there are several great descents and satisfying climbs in the area and the only way to do them the 'right' way round is to hop around a bit. The enjoyable result is one of the more technically difficult rides in the book. Yeah, there's a bit of road along the way, and you cross your tracks a couple of times (think of these as a built-in short cut options) but the descents more than make up for this. If you're comfortable on tricky ground, you can pick up some serious speed and have a lot of fun. If you're less confident, don't worry — nothing here is unrideable and you'll have a great time picking lines between the rocks. A great ride.

The Ride

The road out of Bisley warms up your legs, but does nothing to prepare you for the first descent. Dropping through the woods above Slad, it's fast and technical from the off. Steep climbing follows, firstly on the road and then up a dirt track. Another, more open descent plummets towards Painswick before the ride turns back on itself, climbing up to a loose and rocky descent. Next, a long, gradual drag, a fair stretch along the road and some easy descending takes you to Edgeworth. A swift descent and a tough climb lead to the steepest descent of the route – a wide, but loose track towards Lypiatt – and a great opportunity to scare yourself silly! A big road climb sees you at a final rocky descent and the last climb – a rubble-strewn challenge. Easy riding runs back to Bisley.

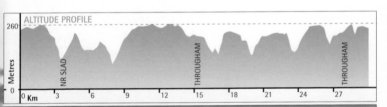

ALTITUDE PROFILE

260

Metres

NR SLAD

THROUGHAM

THROUGHAM

0 Km   3   6   9   12   15   18   21   24   27

BISLEY **GRADE:** ▲

TOTAL DISTANCE: 30KM » **TOTAL ASCENT**: 850M » **TIME**: 3–5 HOURS » **START/FINISH**: STIRRUP CUP INN, BISLEY
START GRID REF: SO 904060 » **SATNAV**: GL6 7BQ » **PARKING**: ON-STREET IN BISLEY, CAR PARK OPPOSITE THE BEAR INN
OS MAP: LANDRANGER 163 & 162 » **PUB**: THE BEAR INN, BISLEY, TEL: 01452 770 265; THE STIRRUP CUP INN, BISLEY,
TEL: 01452 770 280 » **CAFÉ**: SHOP IN BISLEY

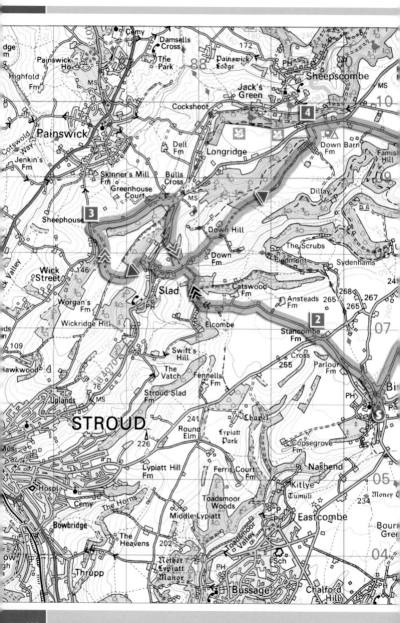

16 BISLEY

Directions – Bisley

➔ With your back to the Stirrup Cup Inn, turn **L** and follow the main road out of the village and keep **L** at the fork, signed *Stroud*.

2 About 1km out of Bisley, take the second **R** as you reach houses, signed *Ansteads Farm* and *Catswood*. After 1.5km, as the road drops into the woods and begins to descend steeply, turn **R** onto a signed byway. Rattle downhill, ignoring turnings and sticking to the main track. At the road, turn **L**. Climb steeply through the village of Slad. As the gradient eases and the road bends left, turn **R** and keep climbing. Go **SA** over the main road and climb the short lane, moving onto dirt as the road ends. Follow the track around the top of the hill and descend the wide track to the road.

3 Turn **R** and climb the road. Keep **R** at the fork and then turn **R** onto a rocky track. Go **SA** at the top and turn **R** onto the road. 100m after the Slad boundary sign, turn **L** onto a wide track. Rattle down to the road and turn **L**. As the road ends, go through the gate into the field. Keep **L** and climb the obvious track into the woods. Turn **L** as you reach a minor lane and ride to the main road.

4 Turn **R**, and then take the first **R**, signed *The Camp*. At the crossroads, turn **R**. After 400m turn **L**, following signs for Througham. Turn **L** opposite the barns, keep **R** at the fork and turn **R** at the junction. Follow the road out of the houses, around to the left and turn **L** onto a dirt track alongside the fields. Follow this track, ignoring turnings to the road. Turn **L** and pass between buildings onto a dirt track. Drop to the farm and follow the track to the right, passing through gates. At the track T-junction after the second gate, turn **L**.

5 Descend and climb rocky trails to a T-junction. Turn **L** and climb past a barn and out of the woods. After 150m, bear **R** through a gate into more woods. Follow vague tracks out of the trees and around the field edge. Go **SA** over the road and pass between the houses onto a wide track. Continue **SA** through a gate as this bends left and trend **L** across the field to a gate by the house.

6 Follow the lane to a sharp left-hand bend and keep **SA** towards the impressive house. Turn **R** through stone posts just before the house gates. Following bridleway signs, **ride responsibly** through the gardens and drop to a bridge. Climb to the road and turn **R**.

7   At the crossroads, turn **L**. Turn **L** again in front of a large farmhouse. Go **SA** through the gate at the end of the road, cross the field and follow the obvious track into the woods. Stay on this for 500m, ignoring all turnings, and descend to a sharp right-hand corner. Turn **L**, leave the woods and descend steeply on an obvious track through fields.

8   Turn **L** on to the road and climb steeply. Turn **R** at the T-junction (**ignore** the road immediately to your right) and, after 300m, turn **L** onto a signed byway. When this bends right by the cricket club, go **SA** through a gate onto a bridleway. Drop down this and climb to the road.

9   Retracing your steps, ride through Througham and pick up the track you took earlier beyond the houses. Follow this to the first corner and bear **R** through a gate onto a signed byway. Follow this around fields to the road and turn **L**. Go **SA** at the crossroads and ride back to Bisley.

17 Cam & Uley

25km

Introduction

This ride might be short, but it's far from easy. With over 1,000m of vertical ascent, you need to be fit for this ride – particularly since most of that height is gained via some of the hardest climbs in the Cotswolds. But wait... what goes up must also come down and the payback for all that climbing is a vertical kilometre of descent. Rocky, rooty, steep and sketchy – the downhills here are tricky, but there's not a dull trail amongst them. One of the toughest and most technically difficult rides in the guide, you want to be feeling strong and confident to get the most from it. If that's you, get over here – you'll enjoy this.

The Ride

The ride starts innocently, with easy tracks and quiet lanes leading to Hodgecombe Farm. A narrow trail ambles out of the farmyard and then kicks hard uphill on a technically easy but steep climb. Without pausing for breath, it plunges back downhill on a slippery and rutted track through Coaley Wood, where singletrack trails wind to a second, soaring climb. At the top, spin along the road, take a breather at the viewpoint and then drop down a loose, rocky descent. This track dealt me my biggest crash in the Cotswolds, so take care. Road and singletrack lead to the climb from Uley to Bury Ramparts. The hardest climb here, you'll have to ride well to clean this. A tight descent drops to Uley and a road climb leads into Folly Wood. Here, a series of fast descents and long climbs wind west to Stinchcombe and the finale of the ride – steep, singletrack freefalling the entire height of the hill.

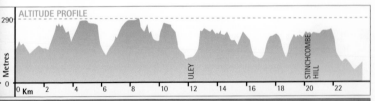

CAM & ULEY **GRADE:** ▲

TOTAL DISTANCE: 25KM » **TOTAL ASCENT:** 1,100M » **TIME:** 3-5 HOURS » **START/FINISH:** PEAKED DOWN CAR PARK
START GRID REF: ST 766993 » **SATNAV:** CAM (NEAREST) » **OS MAP:** LANDRANGER 162
PUB: PUB? THERE'S A BREWERY IN ULEY! TEL: 01453 860 120 » **CAFÉ:** LOTS IN CAM AND DURSLEY

Directions – Cam & Uley

❻► Head uphill, away from the car park, passing immediately **L** of the house. Ride through a small 'valley' and follow bridleway signs **SA** at the track junction. Turn **R** at the good track and, after 200m, turn **L** across a small bridge. At the road, turn **L**.

❻► **Winter Alternative Start**
Turn **L** out of the car park, towards Cam. Take the first **L** and then, after 200m, **L** again. Rejoin the route at **2**.

2 At the T-junction, turn **L** and take the first **R**, into Hodgecombe Farm. Go through the farmyard onto an initially narrow track and climb steeply as the track widens. Immediately before reaching the gate at the top of the climb, turn sharp **L** onto an obvious track. Drop steeply downhill, forking **L** at the junction onto a technical descent. Drop to the edge of the woods and turn **R** along singletrack. Follow this to a house and bear **R**, following bridleway signs, to climb steeply to the road.

3 Turn **L** along the main road. Follow the road for just over 1km, passing a big picnic spot (stop for a snack – good views!) and turn **L** onto a signed bridleway. Bear **L** at the fork immediately after the gate and descend, ignoring turnings, around corners and through a gate, to the road.

4 Turn **L** and climb to the main road. Turn **R** and, after 700m, turn **L** into a layby at a bridleway sign. Bear **R** across the small open area onto singletrack. **Easy to miss:** After 200m, fork **L**, still on singletrack. Drop through the woods and keep **R** at the junction. Keep **SA** onto the lane. At the main road, turn **R** and then almost immediately **L** onto a narrow bridleway.

5 At the top, go through the gate and climb the obvious track to the top of Bury Ramparts. Turn sharp **L**, back on yourself. Follow the grassy track along the side of the ramparts to a small bridleway marker. Drop down singletrack and turn **L** through a narrow gate. Descend to the road and turn **L**.

6 Ignoring turnings, follow the road into Uley. Go **SA** at the crossroads. After 900m, bear **R** onto a signed bridleway and climb steeply into the woods.

DIRECTIONS CONTINUE ON PAGE 108

STROUD DISTRIC

17 CAM & ULEY

7 Go **SA** over the track crossroads and continue climbing. Head out of the woods through a gate and, following bridleway signs, trend **R** through gates, soon re-entering the woods.

Note: *Giving directions through woods is tricky as there are often lots of unmarked tracks and 'Turn left by the oak' rarely helps... In this case it's easy to stray off the bridleway onto singletrack. If you do go wrong, check the map – the woods are narrow and a road runs along their upper edge – keep heading west, be aware of the position of the road and you'll be ok.*

Following hoof prints and tyre tracks, keep **SA** at the junction and drop through the woods. Follow the obvious track as it runs along the bottom of the woods and then begins to climb. Turn **R**, now following bridleway markers and descend towards fields and a house. Turn **L**, staying in the woods past the house and then turn **L** to climb a wide track.

8 At the top, turn **R** onto a wide track. Follow this downhill. Keep **SA/slightly L** at the track junction, and follow a wide gully out of the trees onto singletrack running through fields. Follow farm tracks to the road and turn **L**.

9 At a sharp left-hand bend, turn **R** onto a bridleway by chevron signs. Climb steeply and then trend **L** through bombholes. Follow the main track (bridleway signs/blue paint on trees) **SA** through the weird art installations to the road. Turn **R** onto a signed bridleway and keep **R** at the fork. Drop downhill, ignoring turnings, go around steep rocky corners and follow the track out of the woods. Go **SA** on to the road and turn **L** at the junction.

10 Go **SA** at the end of the road onto a wide track and, ignoring turnings, climb through the woods. At the top of the hill, turn **R** along a wide, flat track. Follow this to a clearing and bear/turn **L** across it on to another wide track running along the top of the woods briefly alongside a field. Follow the track, marked by blue paint on trees **SA** to the road. You should pop out on a road descending from left to right. Turn **L** and then **R** at the T-junction.

Note: If you accidentally leave the woods early, you'll find yourself on the relatively flat road running along the top of the woods. Turn R.

11 As you reach open grassland, bear **R** alongside the edge of the grass and follow bridleway markers past the golf clubhouse and around the edge of the course. Follow markers to a bridleway junction by a bench and turn **R**. Drop steeply, ignoring turnings, and keep **SA** at junctions, through the woods. Take care near the houses and, at the road, turn **R**.

12 Turn **R** at the roundabout and then turn **L** just after Somerfield, onto Kingshill Lane. Follow this around sharp left- and right-hand corners and up a short climb before turning **R** onto Springhill just after a phone box. Climb out of the houses, ignoring turnings, and follow the road back to the car park.

18 Wotton-under-Edge

Introduction

One of the longer rides in the book, this isn't an easy ride. Tracing a big loop through the south-west Cotswolds, it makes the most of the hilly surroundings with over 1,200m of descent! With downhills ranging from fast, open trails to steep singletrack and technical rocky tests, there's a lot of fun to be had. However, don't forget that you've got to go up to come down, and the climbs here are steep and tricky to ride without a dab. So make sure you're feeling fit if you want to get the most from this route!

Note: If you don't fancy the full 40km ride, you can return to Wotton via the marked short cut (taking in an excellent, if short, singletrack descent) to complete a 21km route, or head out along the short cut to take in the more challenging second half of the route and create a 25km ride.

The Ride

Head south out of Wotton on the road. Hang a left, speed downhill on wide trails and then turn north for a long climb to Tresham. Fly along the road, rattle down to Ozleworth Bottom on a rocky trail and tackle the tricky climb out. Drop fast, back into Ozleworth and climb out past the park. Take the road north towards Uley (and the short cut home – should you want it) and turn left into Folly Wood. Dart up and down the hillside above Dursley on a number of stonking descents and tough climbs and then drop off the end of Stinchcombe Hill on steep singletrack. Grunt back up to the top, zip down the southern side of the hill and follow roads and easy climbs to North Nibley. Climb to the Knoll, play about in the woods and then take the fast singletrack descent back to Wotton.

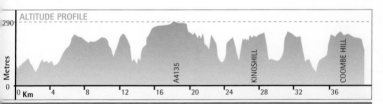

ALTITUDE PROFILE

WOTTON-UNDER-EDGE   GRADE: ▲

TOTAL DISTANCE: 21 OR 40KM » **TOTAL ASCENT**: 1,200M » **TIME**: 4–7 HOURS » **START/FINISH**: ROUNDABOUT IN THE CENTRE OF WOTTON » **START GRID REF**: ST 758933 » **SATNAV**: WOTTON-UNDER-EDGE » **PARKING**: CAR PARKS IN WOTTON **OS MAP**: LANDRANGER 162 » **PUB**: THE STAR INN, WOTTON, TEL: 01453 844 651; THE ROYAL OAK, WOTTON, TEL: 01453 842 316 **CAFÉ**: PLENTY IN WOTTON

18 WOTTON-UNDER-EDGE PART 1

STARTS ON PAGE 114

CONTINUES ON PAGE 113

18 WOTTON-UNDER-EDGE PART 2

Directions – Wotton-under-Edge

⑤ From the roundabout in the centre of Wotton, follow signs for Hillesley (bear **R** at the fork and then follow the road past the school and out of Wotton).

2 Follow the road, ignoring turnings and climb into Alderley. Just before the road begins to descend, turn **L** onto a marked byway between houses. Follow this through fields and gates to a T-junction with a wide track and turn **L**. Climb to the road and turn **R**. At the main road, turn **L** and then take the next **L** down a dead end lane. Continue **SA** as the road ends onto a wide track. Go past the big house and through a gate. Drop downhill, turning **R** at the junction towards a small lake.

3 Follow the main track to climb steeply to tarmac. Ride past the houses and turn **L** onto a signed bridleway next to the pigs. Go across fields into the woods. Keep **SA** initially on the main track. As this track bends sharp right, go **SA** onto a narrow, signed bridleway. Drop steeply out of the woods and descend **SA** across the field ahead. Go through a gate and cross the stream. Turn **L** along the main track for a short distance and then turn **R**, following bridleway arrows onto singletrack. Go through a gate into a field and go **SA** to the house and road. Turn **R**.

4 Climb to the road junction and turn **R**, pressing the button by the gate to gain access to the lane beyond. Follow bridleway signs through Newark Park and continue **SA** onto the road. Keep **R** at the fork.* Turn **R** at the T-junction with the main road and then take the next **L**.

*Optional Route – Short Cut
OR Just after a road turning on the right, turn **L** through a gate onto a signed bridleway. Drop into a field and bear **R** to a narrow gate into the woods. Go through the gates and onto a brilliant singletrack descent. Leave the woods and head straight downhill towards the river, bearing **L** as you near it. Cross the river and follow vague tracks along the bottom of the valley, eventually joining a better track. Turn **L** at the road, go **SA** at the junction and follow the road to the centre of Wotton.

5 At the crossroads, turn **L**. When the lane bends right, turn **L** through a gate onto a signed bridleway. Drop into the courtyard of a house and go **SA/bear L** through a gate into fields. Trending downhill and roughly **SA/slightly R**, pass through a second gate then through a third into the woods. Drop to the junction.

Note: *Giving directions through woods is tricky as there are often lots of unmarked tracks and 'Turn left by the oak' rarely helps... In this case it's easy to stray off the bridleway onto singletrack. If you do go wrong, check the map – the woods are narrow and a road runs along their upper edge – keep heading west, be aware of the position of the road and you'll be ok.*

6 Following hoof prints and tyre tracks, keep **SA** at the junction and drop through the woods. Follow the obvious track as it runs along the bottom of the woods and then begins to climb. Turn **R**, now following bridleway markers and descend towards fields and a house. Turn **L**, staying in the woods past the house and then turn **L** to climb a wide track.

7 At the top, turn **R** onto a wide track. Follow this downhill. Keep **SA/slightly L** at the track junction, and follow a wide gully out of the trees onto singletrack running through fields. Follow farm tracks to the road and turn **L**.

8 At a sharp left-hand bend, turn **R** onto a bridleway by chevron signs. Climb steeply and then trend **L** through bombholes. Follow the main track (bridleway signs/blue paint on trees) **SA** through the weird art installations to the road. Turn **R** onto a signed bridleway and keep **R** at the fork. Drop downhill, ignoring turnings, go around steep rocky corners and follow the track out of the woods. Go **SA** on to the road and turn **L** at the junction.

9 Go **SA** at the end of the road onto a wide track and, ignoring turnings, climb through the woods. At the top of the hill, turn **R** along a wide, flat track. Follow this to a clearing and bear/turn **L** across it on to another wide track running along the top of the woods briefly alongside a field. Follow the track, marked by blue paint on trees, **SA** to the road. You should pop out on a road descending from left to right. Turn **L** and then **R** at the T-junction.

Note: *If you accidentally leave the woods early, you'll find yourself on the relatively flat road running along the top of the woods. Turn R.*

DIRECTIONS CONTINUE OVERLEAF

10   As you reach open grassland, bear **R** alongside the edge of the grass and follow bridleway markers past the golf clubhouse and around the edge of the course. Follow markers to a bridleway junction by a bench and turn **R**. Drop steeply, ignoring turnings, and keep **SA** at junctions, through the woods. Take care near the houses and, at the road, turn **L**.

11   Keep **SA** at the road junction, towards North Nibley. After 400m, turn **L** onto a wide bridleway. Tough climbing leads back to the golf course. Follow bridleway signs **L** and then turn **R** onto the track running through the middle of the course. Ride past two car parks and turn **R** in front of the row of houses.

12   Go **SA** into the trees as the tarmac ends and follow the wide track around a left-hand hairpin. Ignoring turnings, follow the track downhill to the road. Turn **R**. At the junction, turn **L**. Just before the road enters woods, turn **R** onto a signed bridleway. Follow this to the road. At the T-junction, turn **L**.

13   At the main road, turn **R**. After 100m, turn **L** onto a signed bridleway. Climb into the woods and follow the main track through the trees into a field. Go **SA** across the field and through a gate on the far side.

14   Once in the trees, keep **L** and follow bridleway signs to a multiple track junction. Bear **L**, again following bridleway signs and continue **SA** over two good tracks until you begin to run parallel to fields on your right. Continue **SA** until the woods narrow and a field appears to the left. Go **SA** onto a wide track running along the edge of the woods, keeping this second field to your left. Follow the track through the woods and across the field to the road. Turn **L**.

15   Go past turnings on the right and left and then turn **R** onto a signed bridleway. Drop steeply down singletrack to the road. Turn **R** to return to Wotton.

SECTION 4

Killers

*They shouldn't actually kill you but
they will certainly wear you out, building
character in the process. Allow plenty
of time, make sure you're well prepared
and fuelled and then have it. Give it
100% and that's what you'll get back –
big rides that reward hard work.*

Killers
sponsored by

www.ibiscycles.co.uk

TOP RIDING NEAR ULEY (ROUTE 19)

Gloucestershire Way
Public Bridleway

19 Nailsworth & Wotton-under-Edge   59km

Introduction

At almost 60km in length, with 1,600m of climbing and some tricky descents, this is a big ride. Running from Naunton to Wotton-under-Edge, the first half of the route is relatively flat, running along easy tracks through farmland. Don't get carried away here – you need to save energy for the big climbs in the second half of the ride. Beginning first near Wotton, these climbs are generally not technical, but are steep and demand determination to ride cleanly. The descents, ranging from the steep singletrack of Stinchcombe Hill to the slippery trails near Uley and the final drop to Nailsworth, are all great fun, and a just reward for the effort put in to reach them. As with any Cotswold ride of this length, there are a few road miles to be covered along the way, but don't worry – you're in a beautiful part of the country, so sit back and enjoy the ride.

The Ride

Leave Nailsworth and quickly gain height on road and easy bridleways. Follow good tracks to a short drop into Avening and then cruise through open countryside via easy bridleways, singletrack and quiet roads towards Ozleworth. As you get there, rattle down a fast, often wet descent, grind up the climb and drop through the woods. Spin along the road, enjoy the singletrack switchbacks into Tyley Bottom and then climb out of Wotton. A fast singletrack descent leads to easy tracks past Nibley Knoll, from where more easy riding and a tough climb heads to the top of Stinchcombe Hill. Hurtle down this on singletrack and clamber up to Bury Ramparts above Uley. Enjoy a couple of superb descents, pretend to enjoy a leg-burning climb and then check out the countryside as you cruise along roads and through pleasant woodland. Finish off by diving through the woods on a twisting and turning descent to Nailsworth.

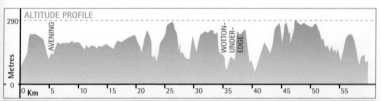

ALTITUDE PROFILE

290 — Metres — 0

AVENING

WOTTON-UNDER-EDGE

0 Km   5   10   15   20   25   30   35   40   45   50   55

NAILSWORTH & WOTTON-UNDER-EDGE   GRADE: ▲

TOTAL DISTANCE: 59KM » **TOTAL ASCENT**: 1,600M » **TIME**: 5 HOURS+ » **START/FINISH**: NAILSWORTH CLOCK TOWER
START GRID REF: ST 850997 » **SATNAV**: NAILSWORTH » **PARKING**: PLENTY OF CAR PARKS IN NAILSWORTH
OS MAP: LANDRANGER 162 & 163 » **PUB**: LOTS TO CHOOSE FROM » **CAFÉ**: LOTS OF CHOICE

CONTINUES ON PAGE 129

**19 NAILSWORTH &
WOTTON-UNDER-EDGE
PART 1**

CONTINUES ON PAGE 126

19 NAILSWORTH & WOTTON-UNDER-EDGE
PART 2

Directions – Nailsworth & Wotton-under-Edge

➌ With your back to the clock tower beside the mini roundabout at the bottom of Nailsworth, go **SA/L** onto the A46/Bath Road, heading towards Tetbury and Wotton Climb carefully – this is a busy road – away from the houses for about 1km before forking **L** up a narrow, signed bridleway. Go **SA** along the lane onto a wide track Turn **L** at the T-junction and follow the wide track into the woods.

2 Follow the track as it bends **R** on the far edge of the woods. Leaving the trees, bear **L** onto a narrower trail alongside the field. Drop to the lane and follow it to a T-junction. Turn **R** and climb steeply to a sharp right-hand bend by a small shop. Continue **SA** onto a minor road and then turn **R** after 100m. As the lane bends left, turn **R** onto the left-hand of the two tracks. Follow this to the road.

3 Turn **R**. Go **SA** at the crossroads and turn **L** at the T-junction at Chavenage Green. After 400m, turn **R** as you approach the houses and ride past barns into fields. Follow bridleway signs and obvious tracks through the small woods. Turn **R** then immediately **L** (in effect **SA**) at the main road and continue **SA** up the field ahead and, at the road, turn **R**. Keep **R** at the junction and go **SA** at the crossroads.

4 Follow the road through Leighterton, going **SA** at all junctions. Leave the village and go **SA** over the main road onto a dead end lane. Continue **SA** as the road ends, onto a wide track. Go past the big house and through a gate. Drop downhill, turning **R** at the junction towards a small lake. Following the main track, climb steeply to tarmac. Ride past the houses and turn **L** onto a signed bridleway next to the pigs. Go across fields into the woods. Keep **SA** initially, on the main track. As this track bends sharp right, go **SA** onto a narrow, signed bridleway. Drop steeply out of the woods and descend **SA** across the field ahead. Go through a gate and cross the stream. Turn **L** along the main track for a short distance and then turn **R**, following bridleway arrows onto singletrack. Go through a gate into a field and go **SA** to the house and road. Turn **R**.

5 Climb to the road junction and turn **R**, pressing the button by the gate to gain access to the lane beyond. Follow bridleway signs through Newark Park and continue **SA** onto the road. Keep **R** at the fork. Follow the lane for 1.25km and turn **L** onto a signed bridleway, shortly after a turning on the right. Drop into a field and bear **R** to a narrow gate into the woods. Go through the gates and onto a brilliant singletrack descent. Leave the woods and head straight downhill towards the river, bearing **L** as you near it. Cross the river and follow vague tracks along the bottom of the valley, eventually joining a better track.

6 At the road, turn **R**. Keep **R** at the junction and climb to the main road. Go **SA** onto obvious singletrack and climb steeply to the road. Go **SA** onto a signed bridleway and descend fast. At the road, turn **L** and climb steeply to a T-junction. Turn **R**.

7 Shortly after a wide dirt parking area on the right, turn **R** onto a signed bridleway. Follow this into the woods and bear **R** up the wide trail, keeping the field to your left. As the field ends, continue **SA** into the woods and follow the obvious trail and bridleway signs, bearing slightly **R** and crossing **SA** over two good tracks. Continue **SA/bear slightly R** at the multi track junction and follow the bridleway out into the field.

8 Go **SA** across the field and through the gate on the far side. Follow the obvious track **SA** and drop to the road. Turn **R** and then take the next **L**. Take the second **R** in front of a bench. Keep **SA** onto the bridleway and follow this down to the road. Turn **L**, then, after 750m, turn **R**. Just after the road bends right, turn **L** and follow the track into the woods.

9 Climb the obvious track. As the gradient eases, turn **R** around a hairpin and, keeping to the wide track, ride out of the woods and to the road. Cross the road and bear **L** to follow bridleway signs and markers past the golf clubhouse and around the edge of the course. Follow markers to a bridleway junction by a bench and turn **R**. Drop steeply, ignoring turnings and keeping **SA** at junctions, through the woods. Take care near the houses and, at the road, turn **R**.

10 Turn **R** at the roundabout and then turn **L** just after Somerfield, onto Kingshill Lane. Follow this around sharp left- and right-hand corners and up a short climb before turning **R** onto Springhill Close just after a phone box. *Climb out of the houses, ignoring turnings, and, just after a sharp left-hand bend, bear **R** onto a signed bridleway.

DIRECTIONS CONTINUE OVERLEAF

*Optional Route – Winter alternative

▶OR▶ Climb out of the houses and take the first lane on the **R**. After 200m, turn **L**. Rejoin the route at **12**.

11 Continue roughly **SA**, aiming for the house above the car park. Pass to the **L** of the house and then keep **R**. Ride through a small 'valley' and go **SA** at the track junction, following bridleway signs. Turn **R** at the good track and then turn **L** across a small bridge after 200m, as the main track turns right. At the road, turn **L**.

12 Go **SA** over the lane onto a wide track. Keep **R** on this track and climb through a gate onto open ground. Follow singletrack **SA** and then **L**. At the top of the hill, turn **R** (in effect roughly **SA**) along the side of the old ramparts. Go around the left-hand corner at the far end and then turn sharp **R** back on yourself to descend an obvious track to a gate. Go through this and drop down the technical descent to the road. Turn **L** and climb until you reach a parking area on your left as the road bends right. Go **SA** off the road through the gate. Turn **R** to drop steeply downhill, forking **L** at the junction onto a technical descent. Drop to the edge of the woods and turn **R** along singletrack. Follow this to a house and bear **R**, following bridleway signs, to climb steeply to the road.

13 Go **SA** over the main road onto a lane. Follow this for 3.5km and turn **R** (in effect **SA**) at the junction. Shortly afterwards, turn **L** onto a wide track.

14 Go past the buildings and then turn **L** just beyond them, following bridleway arrows through a gate into the woods. Take the increasingly obvious track out to the road. Turn **L**, then **R** at the T-junction. Almost immediately, turn **R** again, drop steeply to the river and climb to the main road.

15 Go **SA** onto a narrow lane and follow this, retracing your tyre tracks briefly, through the woods. As the track bends sharply to the right on the far side of the woods, go **SA**, along the field edge and continue **SA** over the track junction onto a brilliant descent. At the road, turn **L** and then **R** opposite the pub. Climb steeply uphill before turning **L** to return to the clock tower.

20 Winchcombe Beast

Introduction

What a ride! Essentially combining three of the more technical routes in this guide, two of which contain some serious hills and difficult riding, this is hard. It gives a taste of everything the north Cotswolds has to offer – rocky descents, rooty trails and fast open farm tracks. There are expansive views (out towards Wales on a good day), some nice little villages (with some nice little pubs) and plenty of good riding. This isn't a ride you're going to want to be doing in winter – it's hard enough in the summer, without an extra 20lbs of winter mud clogging your wheels. There are mud-avoiding routes marked on the map, but they're for 'marginal' rather than truly muddy days. Finally, there are a couple of obvious short cuts if you don't fancy the full distance.

The Ride

The ride kicks off with a big climb from Winchcombe. This is followed by an enjoyable fast and rocky descent and then a second, swoopier downhill – with stiff, but technically easy climbs to regain the lost height. A respite from climbing follows as flat, easy tracks and quiet lanes head south towards the central Cotswolds. A hidden section of singletrack, a wide valley, a sharp climb and cheeky descent lead to the village of Naunton. From here, easy off-road and quiet on-road riding amble through open countryside to Cleeve Hill – the highest point of the Cotswolds. Clamber up, admire the stunning views and drop off the hill on a brilliant descent through the trees. A slog up the road follows – but this is now the home straight, so dig deep and get it done. The final descent starts innocently, but grows rockier and faster until it's a full on tooth-rattling blast down to Winchcombe.

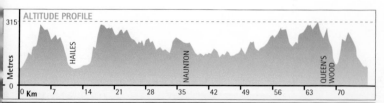

WINCHCOMBE BEAST   **GRADE:** ▲

TOTAL DISTANCE: 77KM » **TOTAL ASCENT**: 1,850M » **TIME**: A LONG TIME! » **START/FINISH**: T-JUNCTION IN WINCHCOMBE
START GRID REF: SP 025283 » **SATNAV**: WINCHCOMBE » **PARKING**: PAY AND DISPLAY IN WINCHCOMBE
OS MAP: LANDRANGER 150 & 163 » **PUB**: WHITE HART, WINCHCOMBE, TEL: 01242 602 359; ROYAL OAK, GRETTON,
TEL: 01242 604 999; LOTS MORE IN WINCHCOMBE » **CAFÉ**: JURI'S TEA ROOM, WINCHCOMBE, TEL: 01242 602 469;
SEVERAL MORE IN WINCHCOMBE

CONTINUES ON PAGE 138

**20 WINCHCOMBE
BEAST** PART 1

CONTINUES ON PAGE 140

20 WINCHCOMBE BEAST PART 2

20 WINCHCOMBE BEAST PART 3

Directions – Winchcombe Beast

❺▸ From the T-junction in the centre of Winchcombe, turn **R**, towards Cheltenham, and then take the first **L**, onto Castle Street. Climb out of Winchcombe, turning **R** after 1.5km onto a lane to Sudeley Lodge. Keep **L** past the farm buildings and continue to climb on a wide track. At the road, go **SA** onto a bridleway. Follow this to the road and turn **L**.

2 After 100m, turn **R** onto a narrow, signed bridleway to the left of the gates. Turn **L** at the road and then take the next **R**. As the lane ends, continue **SA** onto a wide track and rattle down a rocky descent. Continue **SA** onto the road and turn **R** at the junction. At the main road, turn **R** and then immediately **R** again, towards Didbrook. Follow the road to a crossroads with the B4077.

3 **Take care** – this can be busy. Turn **R**, signed to Stow. After 1km, bear **L** off the main road at a group of houses. Go **SA** between buildings onto a narrow bridleway marked *No Motor Vehicles*. Follow the bridleway to a multi-track junction near a stone hut. Turn **R**, (the third track, counting rightwards from the hut) climbing the obvious wide track. Keep **R** (in effect SA) at the next junction, climb, and bear left to leave the woods near a stone barn.

4 As the woods end, bear **L** through a gate and follow the bridleway across fields. Pass through another two gates, turning sharp **L** immediately after the second gate (third gate in total) through a double gate and follow the low stone wall to a farm. Turn **R**, pass through the farm and turn **R** after the cattle grid. Follow this to the road and turn **L** onto an obvious track (**not** straight ahead – you're coming back up here later). Pass through a gate and drop to the village of Stanton. Follow the main road through the village, turning **R** at the T-junction. At the main road, turn **R** and take the first **R**, towards Laverton. Go through the village to a wide byway. Climb this to a T-junction and turn **R** on a good track.

DIRECTIONS CONTINUE OVERLEAF ▶

5 Follow the track on to tarmac. Turn **L** along the lane and then quickly turn **R** onto a grassy bridleway. Follow this through gates and along field edges to the road. Turn **R** and keep **SA** at the junction. At the T-junction with the main road, go **SA** onto a wide track. Follow this into the trees and then continue **SA** through a gate as the main track bends left. Turn **L** at the road and then **R** at the junction. Retrace your steps for 400m, turning **L** at the next road junction and then continue along the lane. Keep **L** at the junction and climb steeply. Continue **SA** onto a wide track as the road swings left. At the road, turn **R**.

6 Drop downhill and cross the river. Climb through a gate and turn **L** onto a dirt track past a small car park. At the T-junction, turn **L** and drop downhill, keeping **R** at the bottom of the short descent. Follow the track to a lane, ride this to a T-junction and turn **L** into Guiting Power.*

*Optional Route – Short cut

OR Follow the road into the village. Turn **R** just after the village green, and then take the next **R**. Pick up the directions midway through **10**. Follow the road through the village. Turn **R** at the T-junction and then take the next **L**.

7 Turn **R** at the next junction, following signs for Naunton. Then take the fourth **R** and immediately turn **L** through a gate onto a grassy bridleway. Follow this, parallel to the road, through gates and across a farm entrance lane. At the end of the bridleway go **SA** across the main road and through a gate onto a wide track. Follow this past a barn, through gates and across fields. At the road, turn **L** and then turn **R** onto a wide signed bridleway opposite the house.

8 At the road, keep **R** and climb above the river and ford. Turn **R** at the triangular junction and **L** at the T-junction. After 1km, turn **R** onto a signed bridleway opposite a road turning. Go **SA** over the road into a field and bear diagonally **R**. Turn **L** after the gate and drop to a track T-junction. Turn **R** and go **SA** for a short distance up the road before turning **R** into Aston Farm (signed).

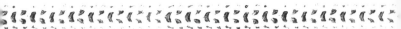

9 Go through the farm and follow vague tracks across the field beyond. Go into the woods and follow wide singletrack, ignoring turnings. Cross a field and turn **L** after the gate on the far side. Follow singletrack down into the valley and keep **SA** along a vague grassy track along the valley floor. Go **SA** over the road onto more vague tracks through gates and fields. After crossing a small stone bridge, climb steeply up the obvious track. Pass the golf course to your left and go **SA** across the road. Go through a gate and drop down singletrack and a wider track to the road. Turn **L** at the T-junction.

10 Climb out of Naunton and turn **R** onto the main road. Follow this for 700m before forking **R** towards Hawling. Drop downhill for a short distance before turning **L** onto a bridleway. Follow this, ignoring turnings, until you drop to the stream. Turn **L** and follow the bridleway to the road. Turn **L**.

11 At a crossroads by houses, turn **R** and follow the lane onto a bridleway. Continue **SA** through fields to the road and turn **L**. Continue **SA** at the crossroads, keep **L** at the next road junction and then go **SA** over the next crossroads onto a dead end road. Just before reaching a gate, turn **L** onto a wide, signed bridleway and follow this across the field and into the woods. Climb to a small car park and turn **R** onto a wide, muddy track.

12 Almost immediately, turn **L** through a gate into a grassy field. After 400m, turn **L** through a second gate and ride along field edges (muddy in winter) to join a wide track. Ignoring turnings, follow this to the road. Turn **R** and, after 500m, turn **L** through a gate onto a signed bridleway running into the nature reserve. Admire the view for a minute and then drop around the woods on obvious tracks. Swing to the **R** around a large switchback and go **SA** through the gate. At the T-junction, turn **L** and continue to descend.

DIRECTIONS CONTINUE OVERLEAF

Directions – Winchcombe Beast
continued...

13 **Very easy to miss:** After about 75m, turn **R** onto singletrack. If you hit a technical rocky section of track, you've missed the turning, so hang a U-turn and have a more careful look. Climb singletrack to a multi-track junction. Go **SA**, crossing the gully, and continue climbing, following bridleway signs, to a gate.

14 Go through the gate and keep **L**, hugging the fence. Bear **L** down the obvious rocky descent and trend **L** across the plateau*, following vague tracks to a gate leading into the woods. Fly or squelch, depending on season, down an entertaining descent to the road.

*Optional Route – Short cut

> Keep **R** across the plateau, crest a small rise and turn **R** onto the obvious track behind the houses. Follow this to a small car park by a cattle grid and rejoin the directions at **16**.

15 **Take care** – the road can be busy. Turn **R** and climb for 1km to the Rising Sun pub. Turn **R** immediately before this onto Rising Sun Lane and cross the cattle grid into a small car park. Turn **L**.

16 Follow good tracks across the grassy common. Keep **R** past the lone building up a short, steep rise and follow the obvious track past the golf course. Keep **SA** through the gate. At a T-junction after a second gate turn **L**, pass through a third gate and rattle down to join the main road. Turn **R** to Winchcombe.

SECTION 5

Bonus Section

» *Leckhampton Hill*
» *Forest of Dean*
» *Top Tens*

Bonus Section
sponsored by

www.rab.uk.com

SINGLETRACK THROUGH BROADWAY WOOD, NEAR SNOWSHILL

Leckhampton Hill

Leckhampton Hill, just south of Cheltenham, is home to some of the most technical riding in the Cotswolds. Popular with all sorts of riders, it is best known for downhilling. Predominantly on narrow, 'natural' trails, the runs are littered with roots and steep corners. This makes them technically difficult to ride (especially in the wet), but also allows plenty of creative lines to be hunted out, making the trails particularly addictive. As you move down the hill, a few of the trails steepen and widen, picking up speed as they run towards a couple of massive jumps. A brilliant place to ride, Leckhampton is well worth a visit. Or two.

Note: *the downhill runs here are not closed and are shared with other user groups – so stay in control and keep an eye out.*

The trails here only exist thanks to the hard work of Cheltenham & County Cycling Club, the Friends of Leckhampton Common and the landowner, Cheltenham Borough Council. The area is a Site of Special Scientific Interest and a management plan has been drawn up to control and protect riding in the area. Please ride responsibly, obey any signs and check the notice board at the car park for up-to-date information. For more information, to read the rules for riding here or to help maintain the trails, check out the websites listed opposite.

Getting there

Leckhampton Hill is just south of Cheltenham. From the roundabout where the A417 meets the A436 by the Air Balloon pub, head east on the A436 and immediately turn L on to a minor road signed *Leckhampton* and *Cheltenham*. Just after 2 miles, as you begin to enter the town, turn R up Daisy Bank Road. Park in the small car park on the right.

Grid Ref: **SO 949188**
Sat Nav: **GL53 9QQ**
Facilities: **Car parking**

For more information go to:
www.thecorrective.com
www.cc-cc.co.uk

Forest of Dean

Hop over the M5 from the Cotswolds and you'll find yourself in the Forest of Dean. You'll also find a wealth of good riding. Grab a map and discover wide forest tracks and sections of tight singletrack, or head to the FODCA trail for a 5km waymarked loop on technical singletrack and a load of downhill runs.

FODCA Trail

A short but surprisingly tricky XC loop. Entirely singletrack, it features a few smooth and fast sections, but also a lot of tough, rooty riding. Line choice is critical, particularly through the corners and on some of the short but tough descents and climbs you'll find along the way. Short but sweet.

Other riding

The Forest of Dean contains mile upon mile of good singletrack, so go and explore. For families and those looking for an easier ride, there are plenty of wide, well-surfaced trails. If you're after the exact opposite, head straight up the hill past the FODCA and you'll find downhill runs left, right and centre. They are all short, yet tricky, feature some tight corners, rooty sections and big jumps.

Getting there

From the Cotswolds, you can get into the Forest of Dean from either the north or south. To get there from the south, take the M5 towards Bristol, then take the M4 and M48 west across the Severn Crossing before turning north up the A48. From the north, cross the M5 at J11a, follow signs for Ross on Wye through Gloucester and then turn south onto the A48. There are car parks throughout the forest.

The FODCA Trail is just north of the crossroads between the B4226 and the B4234 in the Forest of Dean. At the crossroads, head north on the B4234 and turn left after a couple of hundred metres, into what appears to be Gloucestershire Highway's Cannop Depot – the car park is beside the depot.

Grid Ref: **SO 608118**
Sat Nav: **GL16 7EH**
Facilities: **Pay and display parking; toilets; showers; bike shop; bike hire; cafe.**

For more information go to:
www.fodca.org.uk

top 10
Climbs

Surely an oxymoron. Anyway, if you enjoy the challenge, or the opportunity to push yourself on what can only truly be offered by a tough climb, read on. These are the most satisfying climbs in the Cotswolds, listed roughly in order of difficulty...

Uley to the Ramparts
Route 17 – GR ST 789989

Tough to ride dab-free, this is a long, relatively steep and slippery challenge. Dig deep for the steep rocky step at the halfway point!

Coaley Wood
Route 17 – GR SO 790002

This looks more like a wall than a climb. Wide and technically easy, this is a real leg-burner.

Ozleworth Bottom
Route 18 – GR ST 808929

Completely rideable with luck, this is the sort of steep and technical climb that'll punish a moment's lapse in concentration. A solid challenge.

Stinchcombe Hill
Route 18 – GT ST 735991

Seemingly wide and easy, it's a combination of the length, the gradient and the tricky little rock gardens that'll catch you out here.

Lypiatt to Througham
Route 16 – GR SO 924080

There's a good descent on the way from Lypiatt to Througham, but it's followed by this loose, rocky and wet climb to the houses. It looks improbable, but turns out to be surprisingly rideable. Satisfying.

South Hill
Route 14 – GR SO 945164

Not hard and not steep, this is a pleasantly rocky amble up from the road towards Shab radio masts.

Sudeley Lodge
Route 20 – GR SP 039275

A steep pull on the road, a bit of respite on a farm lane and then a big effort up a broken up, loose track. Check out the views behind you!

Bredon Hill
Route 5 – GR SO 991383

A rocky start and a steep grassy middle section gain an easy finish with views stretching for miles in every direction.

Golf course climb near Naunton
Route 9 – GR SP 118226

A 100m long track that has small dog syndrome! With steep and grassy climbing up a 1 in 5 incline – this hurts!

Down Hill
Route 16 – GR SO 878078

Not hard – a steep section up a quiet lane, a slightly easier stretch through fields and then a pleasant cruise through woodland.

1 Leckhampton Hill
Bonus Route – GR SO 951186

It had to be number one really...

2 Coaley Wood
Route 17 – GR ST 786994

Accelerate rapidly down the easy top section, fork left and braaaaake(!) as you hit the ruts, roots and leaves of the lower half.

3 Bredon Hill North Side
Route 5 – GR SO 974395

High speed, mud and roots. Irresponsibly-slippery fun.

4 Hailes Wood
Route 15 – GR SP 058294

Signs at the top 'warn' of a *"water-damaged byway"*... Fast, wet and rocky.

5 Slad East
Route 16 – GR SO 880073

Rough. Rocky. Wet. This is hard, especially when taken at speed. Brilliant fun though.

6 Stinchcombe Hill
Route 18 – GR ST 745988

Although there are a lot of superb runs down Stinchcombe, this steep singletrack plunge off the north side is my personal favourite.

top 10
Downhills

Descents in the Cotswolds might be diminutive, but they're still fun. Massively varied in nature, they range from high speed blasts along loose to farm tracks to rocky rattles and muddy slides over roots. Here are a few of the best.

Hazel Wood
Route 12 – GR ST 859989

A multiple-line, rocky, rooty and slippery swoop through the woods. One of the best.

South from North Wraxall
Route 10 – GR ST 821745

Technical singletrack, dropping fast over rocks and roots. Yet another cracker!

Woods near Biddestone
Route 10 – GR ST 844715

Wide and rocky = wide open. Let off the brakes and have some fun. (Or hold back and still have fun – your choice!)

Cleeve Hill
Route 6 – GR MULTIPLE!

Sorry. I couldn't choose. An open blast with awesome views, a rooty slide through the woods or a tooth-rattle down to Winchcombe. You'll find all three on the Winchcombe and Cleeve Hill route.

Coombe Hill
Route 18 – GR ST 764945

Two for the price of one. Head west, and a straight, technical run drops through the woods. Turn around, and smooth singletrack dives towards Wotton.

Singletracks

(Legal) Singletrack in the Cotswolds may be scarce and hard to find, but when you do stumble across it, it's compelling, fast and will leave a lasting impression.

1 Aston Farm Route 9 – GR SP 144214 – SP 136219

Follow narrow, muddy tracks through the woods and across a field before swooping down into the valley on smooth, perfect singletrack.

2 By Brook Route 10 – GR ST 837713 – ST 841717

Essentially a straight line, but with more than enough kinks, humps and general bumps to put a big smile on your face.

3 The Water Parks Route 1 – GR SU 060935 – SU 075940

Over 2km of wide, twisty singletrack between the lakes. Great riding for everyone.

4 Stinchcombe Hill Route 18 – GR ST 745986 – ST 748992

Skip alongside the golf course on fast singletrack before plummeting off the end of the hill on steep, steep trails.

5 Tyley Bottom Route 19 – GR ST 787947 – ST 786948

This short drop through the woods has been shored-up and re-enforced to create a series of tight, steep corners.

South from North Wraxall
Route 10 – GR ST 821745 – ST 822743

So good it goes in twice! One of our Top Ten Downhills, this technical singletrack descent more than deserves a second mention.

Cleeve Common
Route 6 – GR SO 989246 – SO 988250

A sadly short stretch of perfect singletrack climbing (or descending) gently across the side of the hill. Peaceful.

Bredon Hill South
Route 5 – GR SO 952398 – SO 948396

Flow through the woods on wide and gentle singletrack, hopping over roots and logs. Swoopy!

The Wychwood Way
Route 4 – GR SP 340249 – SP 333259

Not singletrack as such, more a narrowing of the byway as it ducks branches and squeezes between trees. Gratifyingly fast and pedally.

Broadway Wood
Route 15 – GR SP 102345 – SP 100346

The downhill run through Broadway Wood is short, but always manages to stay 'dirty' – guaranteeing 'interesting' cornering!

Appendix

Tourist Information Centres

Bourton-on-the-Water .... T: 01451 820 211
bourton.vic@cotswold.gov.uk

Cheltenham .... T: 01242 522 878
E: tic@cheltenham.gov.uk

Chipping Campden .... T: 01386 841 206
E: information@visitchippingcampden.com

Chipping Norton .... T: 01608 644 379
E: chippingnortonvic@westoxon.gov.uk

Cirencester .... T: 01285 654 180
E: cirencestervic@cotswold.gov.uk

Stow-on-the-Wold .... T: 01451 831 082
E: stowvic@cotswold.gov.uk

Stroud .... T: 01453 760 960
E: tic@stroud.gov.uk

Tetbury .... T: 01666 503 552
E: tourism@tetbury.com

Winchcombe .... T: 01242 602 925
E: winchcombetic@tewkesburybc.gov.uk

Food and Drink

For pubs near individual rides, see the information box for that route.

Jolly Brewmaster, Cheltenham .. T: 01242 772 261
Twelve Bells, Cirencester .... T: 01285 644 549
The Plough, Ford .... T: 01386 584 215
Halfway House, Kineton .... T: 01451 850 344
Royal William, Painswick .... T: 01452 813 650
Mount Inn, Stanton .... T: 01386 584 316
The Gumstool Inn, Tetbury .... T: 01666 890 391
The Snooty Fox, Tetbury .... T: 01666 502 436
The Apple Tree, Woodmancote .. T: 01242 673 277
The Woolpack, Slad .... T: 01452 813 429
Blackhorse, Cranham .... T: 01452 812 217
Butchers Arms, Sheepscombe .... T: 01452 812 113
Farmers Arms, Guiting Power .... T: 01451 850 358

Accommodation

A number of the websites listed below have accommodation sections listing hotels, B&Bs, hostels and campsites in the Cotswolds.

Camping

Folly Farm Campsite
T: 01451 820 285 ..... www.cotswoldcamping.net

Far Peak Campsite
T: 01285 720 858 ..... www.farpeakcamping.co.uk

Youth Hostels

Stow YHA, Stow-on-the-Wold
T: 0845 371 9540

Bike Shops

Noah's Ark, Brimscombe
T: 01453 884 738 .... www.noahsark.co.uk

Cheltenham Cycles, Cheltenham
T: 01242 255 414 .. www.cheltenhamcycles.co.uk

Leisure Lakes, Cheltenham
T: 01242 251 505 ..... www.leisurelakesbikes.com

Roylan Cycles, Cheltenham
T: 01242 235 948 .... www.roylancycles.co.uk

Williams Cycles, Cheltenham
T: 01242 512 291 .... www.williams-cycles.com

Ride 24/7, Cirencester
T: 01285 642 247 .... www.ride-247.co.uk

Weather

www.metoffice.gov.uk
www.metcheck.com

Other Publications

Mountain Biking Trail Centres – The Guide
Tom Fenton, Vertebrate Publishing
www.v-publishing.co.uk

South East Mountain Biking – Ridgeway & Chilterns
Nick Cotton, Vertebrate Publishing
www.v-publishing.co.uk

South West Mountain Biking – Quantocks, Exmoor, Dartmoor
Nick Cotton, Vertebrate Publishing
www.v-publishing.co.uk

Wales Mountain Biking – Beicio Mynydd Cymru
Tom Hutton, Vertebrate Publishing
www.v-publishing.co.uk

Useful Websites

www.winchcombecc.org.uk
www.cc-cc.co.uk
www.thecorrective.com (Leckhampton Hill info)
www.cotswold.gov.uk
www.cotswolds.info
www.visitcotswolds.co.uk
www.the-cotswolds.org
www.cotswoldsaccommodation.com

The Local 'Scene'

The Cotswolds has a rather good local cycling 'scene'. If you're new to the area and are looking for people to ride with, try contacting the Cheltenham or Winchcombe cycling clubs (websites above), or asking in the local shops. If you want something a little different, try entering the massively popular HONC (Hell of the North Cotswolds) endurance event. This is a 50 or 100km ride organised annually by the aforementioned clubs and is great fun. Alternatively, Midlands Trailquests (www.midlandtrailquests.co.uk) organise a series of local three-hour orienteering events on bikes.

The Author

The last ten years of Tom's life have revolved around mountain bikes. He went to university for the trails there, picked jobs for their 'riding time allowance' and has only recently bought a car that's worth more than his bikes. This probably hasn't been the best way to plan his life, but it has certainly been fun!

The Photographer

As well as being Vertebrate's Publishing Manager, John Coefield is also an accomplished photographer with images regularly published in a variety of national publications, including Climb Magazine, Climber Magazine and numerous rock climbing guidebooks. John has been riding since a young age and these days divides his time almost equally between riding, rock climbing, photography and his young family. To view more of John's images please visit: **www.johncoefield.com**

Vertebrate Publishing

Mountain Bike Rider (MBR) Magazine called our MTB guides *"...a series of glossy, highly polished and well researched guidebooks to some of the UK's favourite riding spots."*

That's our plan, and we're almost there. We want to provide you - the rider - with well-researched, informative, functional, inspirational and great-looking MTB guidebooks that document the superb riding across the length and breadth of the UK. So if you want to go riding somewhere, you can count on us to point you in the right direction.

We're one of a new breed of independent publishers, dedicated to producing the very best outdoor leisure titles. As well as our series of MTB guidebooks, we have critically acclaimed and bestselling titles covering a range of leisure activities, including; cycling, rock climbing, hillwalking and others. We are best known for our MTB titles, including the bestseller **Dark Peak Mountain Biking**, which **BIKEmagic.com** said was *"far and away the best Peak guide we've come across".*

We also produce many leading outdoor titles for other publishers including the **Mountain Leader** and **Walking Group Leader Schemes** (MLTUK) and rock climbing guidebooks for the **British Mountaineering Council** and the **Fell and Rock Climbing Club**. For more information, please visit our website: **www.v-publishing.co.uk** or email us: **info@v-publishing.co.uk**

MOUNTAIN BIKING GUIDEBOOKS

About the Great Outdoors

The great outdoors is not bottom bracket friendly; beautiful flowing singletrack can give way suddenly to scary rock gardens, hard climbs can appear right at the end of a ride and sheep will laugh at your attempts to clean your nemesis descent. Of course it's not all good news. You'll need a good bike to ride many of the routes in our set of mountain biking guides. You'll also need fuel, spare clothing, first aid skills, endurance, power, determination and plenty of nerve.

Bridleways litter our great outdoors. Our guides, written by local riders, reveal the secrets of their local area's best rides from 6 to 300km in length, including ideas for link-ups and night-riding options. Critically acclaimed, our comprehensive series of guides is the country's bestselling and most respected – purpose-built for the modern mountain biker.

The Guidebooks

Each guidebook features up to 28 rides, complete with comprehensive directions, specialist mapping and inspiring photography, all in a pocket-sized, portable format. Written by riders for riders, our guides are designed to maximise ride-ability and are full of useful local area information.

MOUNTAIN BIKING TRAIL CENTRES THE GUIDE

TOM FENTON

Mountain Biking Trail Centres – The Guide is the only comprehensive guide to the UK's network of purpose-built, off-road mountain biking trails, featuring thousands of kilometres of singletrack, cross country, downhill, freeride and bike park riding at 67 centres across England, Scotland and Wales.

Included are classics such as Dalby, Coed y Brenin and Glentress, lesser-known centres such as Balblair and Coed Trallwm, together with the latest developments including Whinlatter, Rossendale Lee Quarry and many new trails at existing centres.

"This is without doubt the most comprehensive guide of its type available." MBR Magazine, Guidebook of the Month

"67 centres across England, Scotland and Wales are covered so if you're planning some trips, this is a must read before you load the car." BIKEmagic.com

"If you're planning an excursion to any trail centre, this book is a real gem. And if the pictures throughout the book don't inspire you to ride, we don't know what will." Bikeradar.com

"An absolute must for every committed trail rider in the country." planetFear.com

"This guide is essential for upping the quality of life of anyone with a mountain biking gene – just buy it." Adventure Travel Magazine

"If you ride bikes in the UK you simply can't afford to live without this book." Amazon Review

Available from all good book shops, bike shops and direct from **www.v-outdoor.co.uk**

Notes

Notes

Notes